ENGAGING WITH
COMPLEXITY

Tavistock Clinic Series

Margot Waddell (Series Editor)
Published by Karnac Books

Other titles in the Tavistock Clinic Series

Orders

Tel: +44 (0)20 7431 1075; Fax: +44 (0)20 7435 9076
Email: shop@karnacbooks.com
www.karnacbooks.com

ENGAGING WITH COMPLEXITY

Child & Adolescent
Mental Health and Education

Edited by

Rita Harris, Sue Rendall,
& Sadegh Nashat

KARNAC

First published in 2011 by
Karnac Books
118 Finchley Road
London NW3 5HT

British Library Cataloguing in Publication Data

A C.I.P. for this book is available from the British Library

ISBN: 978–1–78049–003–8

Edited, designed, and produced by Communication Crafts

Printed in Great Britain

www.karnacbooks.com

CONTENTS

SERIES EDITOR'S PREFACE

Margot Waddell

Since it was founded in 1920, the Tavistock Clinic has developed a wide range of developmental approaches to mental health which have been strongly influenced by the ideas of psychoanalysis. It has also adopted systemic family therapy as a theoretical model and a clinical approach to family problems. The Clinic is now the largest training institution in Britain for mental health, providing postgraduate and qualifying courses in social work, psychology, psychiatry, and child, adolescent, and adult psychotherapy, as well as in nursing and primary care. It trains about 1,700 students each year in over 60 courses.

The Clinic's philosophy aims at promoting therapeutic methods in mental health. Its work is based on the clinical expertise that is also the basis of its consultancy and research activities. The aim of this Series is to make available to the reading public the clinical, theoretical, and research work that is most influential at the Tavistock Clinic. The Series sets out new approaches in the understanding and treatment of psychological disturbance in children, adolescents, and adults, both as individuals and in families.

This volume, *Engaging with Complexity: Child & Adolescent Mental Health and Education*, takes us beyond the boundaries of the

clinic into the heart of the community and offers a particular perspective on the communal roots of mental health. Each child is the
bearer of family hopes—and fears—for the future and, on starting
school, becomes a member of an institution that is the prime setting
for the meeting of family and societal expectations and requirements. Parents and teachers alike have a belief in their desire to
support individual children's learning and overall development.
Nonetheless, school can be a very difficult place for both children
and teachers, as well as a focus for parental anxiety; coupled with
this, the broader social context of public educational policy, levels
of employment, housing provision, relative deprivation, attitudes
to immigration, and multicultural cities often add to the problems
with which schools are faced.

Recognition of the vital role of schools in promoting mental
health and containing sometimes severe difficulties has in recent
years led to substantial fresh thinking about how mental health
professionals can work in school settings to improve outcomes for
families, pupils, and school staff. The chapters in this book provide
an extremely interesting picture of initiatives across Europe—in
the United Kingdom, Germany, Italy, and Switzerland—that were
reported on at an international conference, the first of its kind. The
writers come from varied professional and theoretical backgrounds,
and the range of ideas—from psychoanalysis, systemic theory,
attachment theory, group relations, organizational development,
educational and clinical child psychology, child psychotherapy,
and sociology—articulates some very fertile points of integration.
This makes it a book with an important place in the Tavistock
Series. It not only includes a strong and grounded representation
of the core ideas that inspire the Tavistock, but also describes, in
a thoroughly down-to-earth and lively way, how such ideas can
be translated into replicable practice. There are many memorable
accounts of interventions within schools and exclusion units and
of multidisciplinary teams and new community institutions. These
bring to life the voice of the child, the value of discourse, and the
intergenerational background of the difficulties that a child may
struggle with at school.

Engaging with Complexity demonstrates the creative potential of
crossing boundaries, widening perspectives, and taking feelings
seriously, even when they are expressed in ways that are difficult

to bear or understand. The editors have succeeded in allowing the authors' individual voices to contribute to a book that will be read with profit not only by clinicians and teachers, but also by parents, by educational theorists and policymakers, and, indeed, by politicians.

ACKNOWLEDGEMENTS

This book owes its existence to a wide range of people, particularly those who presented papers and symposia at a conference held in Paris, in September 2005, entitled "Child & Adolescent Mental Health in Educational Settings". All those who have contributed to this book presented at that conference and have continued to develop innovative ways of working in this area.

Particular thanks to Anne Andronikof; the late Phil Richardson; Nick Temple and Margaret Rustin; Laura Fruggeri; Serge Boimare; Alireza Alfashari; and Vicky Harrison. Thanks also to Gordi Brown who provided the cover illustration and to Margot Waddell whose clear and impressive editorial skills, coupled with extraordinary patience, enabled this book to be completed.

ABOUT THE EDITORS AND CONTRIBUTORS

Simonetta Adamo is professor of clinical psychology at the University of Milan "Bicocca". She is a child & adolescent psychotherapist and has taught on many Tavistock model observation courses in Italy. She has published papers in academic journals internationally and has contributed to and edited many books on topics such as adolescence, young child observation, projects aimed at improving child & adolescent mental health in educational contexts, the "imaginary companion", Asperger's syndrome, and psychotherapy in paediatric oncology wards. For the past fifteen years she has been co-organising tutor of the short course "Working with Disruptive Adolescents" held at the Tavistock.

Yvonne Ayo is a systemic psychotherapist and systemic supervisor based at the Tavistock Centre. She has a specialist interest in issues of race and culture, in particular that of mixed-heritage families. She has undertaken a small research project that explored the extent to which therapists consider the mixed ethnicities of clients, and more recently she is researching mixed ethnicities in step-families using visual methodologies as part of her systemic doctorate.

She also has an interest in community-based work and works in two secondary schools in Camden.

David Fourmy is a chartered educational psychologist with many years of experience in Australia and the United Kingdom. He is currently employed by an Inner London Local Authority Educational Psychology Service and is also a field tutor on the Tavistock's Doctorate in Child, Community and Educational Psychology programme. He was the coordinator of a short-term government-funded project to pilot locality-based multi-agency working in a local community area, and he continues to support the development and implementation of integrated working practices.

Laura Fruggeri is Professor and Chair at the Department of Psychology, University of Parma (Italy), and Senior Faculty Member at the Milan Center of Family Therapy. She has done extensive research into the analysis of the therapeutic process and of the construction of the relationship between families and social agencies. She has published several articles and books in these areas.

Patrice Govaerts is a clinical psychologist and family therapist who graduated from the University of Geneva. He has been working for the Service Educatif Itinérant (Asturales) in Geneva since 2003.

Rita Harris is CAMHS Director of the Tavistock and Portman NHS Foundation Trust. She continues to work as a clinical psychologist and family therapist in a fostering, adoption, and kinship care service within the Trust, specializing in issues of contact for children with parents with whom they no longer live. She has a long record of developing community services in partnership with local authorities and the voluntary sector and involving children and young people in their planning and delivery.

Gillian Ingall is a consultant child & adolescent psychotherapist at the Tavistock and Portman NHS Foundation Trust. She is currently Head of Child Psychotherapy in the Child and Family Department and is involved with both clinical work and training. She was formerly a teacher for many years in inner-city secondary schools and off-site educational projects with troubled and troubling children and young people.

Sadegh Nashat is a consultant clinical psychologist and a systemic psychotherapist at the Tavistock and Portman NHS Foundation Trust. As a training lead, he has developed and delivered a range of child, adolescent, and family mental health programmes aimed at education professionals. He has a special interest in the area of social and school exclusion and in mental health interventions in education settings.

Nupur Dhingra Paiva works as a chartered clinical psychologist in an inner-city community child & adolescent mental health team with the Tavistock and Portman NHS Foundation Trust. Her current interests include wondering about the appropriateness of Western therapy models with non-Western populations; non-Western experiences of motherhood and postnatal distress; and how marginalized populations understand mental health.

Sue Rendall has worked for forty years in the UK public sector as a secondary school teacher and educational psychologist. She was a Professional Advisor for Child & Adolescent Mental Health at the Department for Education and is an associate consultant for a number of independent consultancy organizations. Her consultancy work includes work with schools in special measures and executive coaching to senior leadership staff, and she has worked in Kosova and Belgrade assessing psycho-social training for the International Organization for Migration. She was a Consultant Child & Educational Psychologist at the Tavistock & Portman NHS Foundation Trust for twelve years, where she was Director for Educational Psychology Doctoral Training, and Vice Dean in the Child & Family Directorate. In 2009 she became Visiting Professor in the Department of Health and Human Sciences, University of Essex. She is the author of a number of articles and book chapters, and of a book with Morag Stuart, *Excluded from School* (2005).

Joseph Rieforth is the academic head of the department for psychosocial postgraduate education at the Center for Life Long Learning—C3L—at the Carl von Ossietzky Universität in

Oldenburg, Germany, and the founder and director of the academic training centre for psychotherapy in Oldenburg. His research and lecturing activities include counselling and therapy methods, supervision, mediation and conflict management, psychological health promotion, and postgraduate studies. Besides his academic activities, he works as a psychotherapist for adults and children.

Margaret Rustin is a consultant child & adolescent psychotherapist at the Tavistock Clinic, London. In 1986 she became Organising Tutor of the Tavistock Child Psychotherapy training and Head of Child Psychotherapy. She has served as both Postgraduate Dean and Chair of the Professional Committee.

Elizabeth Scott is a behaviour support teacher and the Co-ordinator for Secondary Learning Mentors in the London Borough of Camden. Following training and developmental work in educational psychology from 2001, she has also been involved in delivering workshops and training sessions in this field both in the Borough of Camden and elsewhere in the United Kingdom and continues to develop the work in schools as part of her Outreach brief. She has also worked as an EBD Outreach teacher in thirty Oxfordshire schools and was a classroom teacher (English and Humanities) and Head of KS3 for twenty years. Before this, she was a primary school teacher for nine years and has lived and worked in the United States as a Fulbright Scholar.

Maureen Smyth is Head of School at New Rush Hall, a high-performing Redbridge special school for children with behavioural, emotional, and/or social difficulties. A former mainstream secondary teacher, she has worked with vulnerable children since 1980. She is passionate about enhancing understanding of the factors that affect behaviour and has collaborated with the Tavistock Centre since 2001.

Mike Solomon is a consultant clinical psychologist at the Tavistock Clinic and at the London Borough of Camden Secondary Behaviour Support Service. He works in a pupil referral unit with young people excluded from mainstream schools, and he also provides training in mental health for education professionals, as well as offering consultancy to schools and education services.

INTRODUCTION

This book represents the bringing together of the richness and variety of ideas shared by some of the contributors to the first European Conference on Child & Adolescent Mental Health in Education Settings, held in Paris in 2005 and hosted by the Tavistock and Portman NHS Foundation Trust. When organizing this event, it was our intention to gather together child mental health and educational professionals from across Europe to share innovative practice. The success and impact of this conference was such that it became the first of what is now a biannual series of events, each taking place in a different European city. Our experience of this conference was that, although there are issues relating to particular cultures and educational systems, there are many shared ideas and experiences across a European context.

Children and young people spend a great deal of their time in schools and other education settings. Consequently those working in such contexts have a huge impact and influence on the development, experiences, and thinking of the children and young people with whom they interact. We believe such professionals need to understand and be curious about the range of influences—such as home and school, and the complex interactions between these—on the lives of children and young people. The promotion of the emotional and psychological well-being of pupils is a shared concern and responsibility. What became evident throughout the conference is that in many European countries schools are predominantly assessed by government and by the public at large by the academic achievement of their pupils—and this is therefore how children and young people understandably often assess their own achievements. For example, teacher training in the United Kingdom is largely subject-led and subject-focused, child development is not a compulsory component in secondary school teacher training, and there is no traditional culture of reflective supervision for teachers. In this context, we are taking reflective practice to mean enabling staff to reflect upon, and be supported with, the emotional impact that work with children and young people can have and how this is effected and mediated by the contexts within which they live. Achieving this involves providing space to pay attention both to understanding the experiences children have had and the impact of these on their development and to the experiences that we as practitioners bring to the work and our ideas and assumptions that have developed from our experiences and affect our responses to the behaviour and development of children. Where a culture of reflective practice is absent, it is understandable that many education professionals feel uninformed and unskilled in even contemplating that they may have an important role to play in promoting the mental well-being and development of children in their care.

Those working in education often report finding it difficult to recognize and identify mental health difficulties in children. They express anxiety about managing and containing these pupils. This is a complex area, and from the chapters in this book and the papers presented at the conference it is, we understand, one that is shared across European settings. Each of the contributors describes working with this complexity. It may be that given a culture of didactic, performance-managed systems, there is a temptation to seek quick, prescribed remedies.

The need to understand the complexity of the development of mental health difficulties for children in education is critical for those working in health services. Many situations require a holistic approach, as demonstrated throughout this book. We believe that a non-reductionist approach can help practitioners to engage with the complex role of schools. This should include helping children to develop psychologically, emotionally, spiritually, socially, and academically. Teaching and learning is fundamentally a matter of relationships—many young people talk about the "good teachers" as being those who are interested in them, who "know" them. They tend not to talk about the teachers' wonderful knowledge of history or science. The teacher who "knows" his or her pupils is most likely to be the teacher who notices changes in behaviour and warning signs of the troubled child. Ignoring such signs is not an option. Having somewhere to take these concerns is essential in providing support to teachers in order to help them create appropriate ways of engaging and working with pupils and their parents. Many teachers may be anxious and frightened of material associated with mental health; an understanding of their own mental well-being and the impact that their own experiences may have on their understanding of the pupils with whom they work may help them to be less fearful and more able to contain their own and their pupils' anxieties. This is an opportunity for educating staff to contribute to the promotion and development of emotional well-being in children and young people, in whose lives they play a major part.

The contributors to this book are experienced mental health and education professionals from different settings across Europe. During the Paris conference and in the discussions that followed, a number of interconnecting themes emerged, and these are embraced within the chapters of the book. The theme of *acknowledging complexity* is central to all the chapters, thus emphasizing that understanding and intervening is multi-layered and never simple. For example, Laura Fruggeri, in chapter eleven, refers to "a larger social and interpersonal network", in which professionals are involved "in complex relationships even when they are not aware of it". Margaret Rustin (chapter one) examines this same theme, emphasizing a complex "matrix of relationships, all of which reciprocally influence each other". The theme is further expanded to include wider cultural influences in chapters by Simonetta Adamo (chapter nine), Rita Harris and Yvonne Ayo (chapter ten), and Sadegh Nashat and Sue Rendall (chapter twelve). The inescapable influence of the wider social and political context is central to the work presented by Simonetta Adamo, detailing an innovative project carried out in Naples, Italy, designed to support a community badly affected by organized crime. She describes how children and families who had been left with feelings of isolation, fear, and suspicion were helped to re-engage with learning and education.

Within the matrix of relationship, Margaret Rustin identifies a need to *recognize and manage painful feelings* that emerge in both professionals and clients. This theme is a key component in work described by many of the authors throughout this book. Gillian Ingall and Maureen Smyth (chapter six) relate how they use work discussion groups for staff to bring out the "difficult and uncomfortable feelings" that arise in their work with challenging pupils. Patrice Govaerts (chapter seven) gives an account of a home-based systemic approach, developed in Switzerland, to support children with developmental disorders and their parents. They show that by creating a therapeutic alliance with children and parents it is possible to facilitate engagement with the wider professional system. In this work, Govaerts describes providing parents with a "receptacle" to explore their violent and aggressive reactions to their child and the opportunity to explore the guilt they may feel because of their response to having a child with a disability. Nupur Dhingra Paiva (chapter two) demonstrates how inner-city schools can provide a secure base for children where cultural struggles can be understood and, through this understanding, be contained. She writes about parents' unresolved grief about the loss of a child, and its impact on their attitude and behaviour towards a later-born child.

We recognize the struggle that can be involved in this aspect of our work, particularly within a culture where the dominant social and political discourse is that of meeting targets within tight timeframes. In our experience, this often leaves little time either for reflection or for the opportunity to work with the feelings that are evoked. Sadegh Nashat & Sue Rendall and Rita Harris & Yvonne Ayo expand these ideas further in their chapters.

A further link that brings coherence to the work presented in this book is the acknowledged importance by all the contributors of the interrelationship of the *multiple systems* within which children live. Mike Solomon (chapter three) describes work within a unit for pupils excluded from mainstream education, and he offers a model for mental health professionals working in such a context. Similarly David Fourmy (chapter eight) describes his experience of developing a multi-agency team to support children and schools in an Inner London context. Both authors alert us to the tensions that can arise from the different underlying assumptions and beliefs of the agencies, all of which are required to work together to meet the needs of these pupils. Joseph Rieforth's example in chapter four of working in the area of conflict resolution within a school setting highlights the importance of working with multiple systems, as well as the need to recognize the influence of these on the present-ing difficulties. Similarly, Laura Fruggeri draws upon her work in Italy to describe the interconnecting relationships that exist in educational contexts and how they impact upon teacher–learner interaction.

Many of the authors pay particular attention to the importance of clarifying and negotiating the *role of the mental health profes-sional* in working within education contexts. David Fourmy, in his description of developing a multi-agency team, refers to the chal-lenges to professional role and identity that can be experienced. He writes about how, during periods of transition and change, professionals may experience feelings of loss in relation to their professional identity and role, and how this can be managed. This example resonates with the importance of managing painful feel-ings wherever they may lie within the system. In our experience, failure to do so seriously impedes effective joint working. Eliza-beth Scott (chapter five) reminds us of how the role of teachers has developed over time, specifically within the United Kingdom. She talks about teachers now needing to be more aware of the emotional component to learning and child development, and the challenges that this presents to the profession. Both Mike Solomon and Nupur Dhingra Paiva also describe the struggles faced by mental health professionals in education contexts and how these may be worked with.

As editors we have been impressed by the range of work de-scribed by the authors to address the complexities of working with multiple systems. We know from our own experience that this way of working is time-consuming and requires the capacity to engage with differences of cultures, languages, priorities, and roles within different professional agencies. Although these professionals face similar issues in their working lives and we have identified some connecting themes, the book also celebrates diversity of thinking and practice across a range of European education settings.

CHAPTER ONE

Passion in the classroom: understanding some vicissitudes in teacher–pupil relationships and the unavoidable anxieties of learning

Margaret Rustin

Two core assumptions of the psychoanalytic understanding of the mind are at the heart of my suggestion that passion cannot be avoided in the classroom. The first of these is that emotions are an inescapable element of the functioning of our minds. The idea of an area of pure rationality, of cognitive activity being quite separate from human feeling, is not sustainable when we face the reality of the unconscious aspects of our mental processes. Sometimes this idea is felt to be an attack on the value of logical thinking, even a blow to our narcissistic investment in the extraordinary rational powers of human intelligence, but I want to propose that recognition of this other form of our mental experience expands our picture of the mind in ways that make it possible to think about things that otherwise remain inaccessible. I also propose that learning is a form of relationship (Youell, 2006). When we think of school learning we think of subjects, facts, curricula, and so on, and of course a child's relationship to the objects of learning is one aspect of my claim. The other is that the teacher–learner relationship underlies the learning process and that it is one that is full of intensity. It concerns giving and receiving, reciprocity, dependence, growth, and conflict—all primary human experiences, which arouse profound feelings.

In this chapter I shall be exploring some of the implications of these twin themes. The broad picture I propose is that for the child to learn, there must be containment of the emotional aspects of his or her life. This means containment both at the individual level of the teacher–student relationship, but, more broadly, also at the level of the organization of the learning task and the school as an institution. Containment is an onion–like phenomenon in structure—many layers are required when the task is the growth of mind, and this is the primary task of the school (Bion, 1962a; Miller & Rice, 1967). The containment that I am describing is that of the anxieties that are inherent in the demands posed by learning—not a repressive process of holding things in to prevent disorder (containment understood as a policing function), but a more fluid and responsive openness to the painful disturbance of learning.

My focus is therefore on both the student's relationship to the learning task and the dynamics of teacher–pupil relationships. The background for thinking about this requires us to envisage the child at school in quite a concrete way. He or she has to find a place among the year-group, both in and outside the classroom, and to make a relationship with teachers and with other adults, and in this human context to engage with all that the formal learning process requires. This is a matrix of relationships, all of which reciprocally influence each other—child to child, child to adult—both of these, of course, with inputs from each direction and child to the learning task. What may be less obvious is that the learning task itself is quite often experienced as presenting the child with the sort of feelings we would more usually expect in a personal relationship between two people. Teachers and others with experience of helping children with specific difficulties in literacy or numeracy often notice just how tormenting the difficult-to-make-sense-of letters, words, and numbers can feel to a child.

Learning and symbolization

This idea needs some exploration and resonates powerfully with observations I have made over the years of my interest in learning. I remember being very struck when I heard an experienced teacher describe the problem she had in adopting a phonic approach to learning to read with one child. She eventually realized with a shock that when she tried to show how the letters CAT could be taken apart and put together to make the word "cat", and used scissors to cut up the word written on a piece of card, the child felt that a real-life cat was being cut to pieces. Her frightened little pupil shivered and hugged his arms around himself tight, as if, perhaps, he felt that a boy too might feel taken to pieces if one starts to chop up words and names. In this example, we get a glimpse of how the young child's unconscious imaginative life can invade the learning task and be a source of acute anxiety.

When I worked as a teacher doing small-group work in an infant and junior school at the beginning of my career, one child showed me vividly how the relationships between numbers, which are at the heart of mathematical concepts, could be a source of trouble. This little boy, a bright-eyed impulsive character who was a great handful in the classroom, loved sums. In my group, he would clamour for a page of them, not because he could always do them, but because he liked me to sit by him while he worked. One day there was a dramatic episode. He had always had trouble with any sum involving the figure 8. I had observed this problem but had not understood it—he himself was 6 years old at the time—and he suddenly began to talk about his intense curiosity about me and my husband and to fantasize about our sexual activities. I was staggered (though the small-group context did lead to all sorts of more intimate conversations taking place and being more or less manageable), and, of course, I also felt a bit embarrassed; however, while talking, my pupil, Owen, was making 8s all over the page. Looking at these shapes I realized that the number probably represented for him in this image an idea of joined-up figures, which he was now talking about. What was extraordinary to me was that once this equation of the figure 8 with his pictures of adult sexual life had been communicated to me, 8 seemed to become thereafter just a numerical symbol in a more ordinary way, and he could cope with it straightforwardly in his maths work. It had been too much mixed up with private meanings and preoccupations, and thus had become unusable as a symbol in mathematics. This confusion now seemed to have been disentangled, through letting me know the basis of the impasse.

This event was an important learning experience for me in two respects. First, I grasped that it had been more helpful to Owen for me to allow this conversation to take place rather than to shut him up because of its inappropriate and disturbing content. Our exchange resolved something for him in his relationship with me so that I could then become his teacher again, and he could be a boy who liked doing sums. It was as if his head had got overfull of thoughts and feelings about me as a person, which interfered with what we were supposed to be doing, and he had to find a way to sort out this muddle. It is, of course, a delicate matter to know how much to allow this kind of thing to happen within school, but I think that I had a conviction that Owen really urgently needed to say what he said. He could be a very dramatic boy, acting out and acting up to ensure that all the other children in the group were focused on him and on how I was going to deal with his provocative behaviour. On this occasion, by contrast, he was talking in a rather quiet voice to me, and the outburst was not intended to draw in the others. Second, I found in my small-group work that once the group was established as a group and felt they had a reliable place with me, they could be very respectful and even generous about the particular needs of each child. This rather took me by surprise, as I had anticipated more competitiveness for my attention, given the considerable neediness of this group of children. However, it seemed that the school's provision of the opportunity to be in a small group every day for half the morning had served to contain the more infantile aspects of the children—the extra attention they received helped them to cope a bit better in the class for the rest of the day, and their appreciation of being given something more seemed to mitigate the need to compete for attention all the time. It was a bit like a group of siblings where one is allowed to be the baby for the moment and the others feel bigger and more mature temporarily (Canham & Emanuel, 2000).

What I wish to emphasize about this episode in Owen's life at infant school is the relational aspect of his experience. He has an important relationship with me—a rather intense one, both because of his immaturity and because of the small-group context, which elicits this more strongly than the classroom—as well as a relationship to the nature of what we are working on and a relationship to the other children in the room. These three factors need to be vertices of observation in trying to think about all work with children in the school context. It is greatly illuminating if we take into account the inner meaning of external events for all of the actors within the context we are studying. It is both helpful and necessary, especially to understand children with difficulties at school, to try to distil the emotional pressures operating in each of these relationships.

Where home and family background life fit into the child's response to school is a question I shall return to, but perhaps it would be helpful to add just a little about Owen's circumstances, which I was aware of and which are relevant. He was a child of the 1950/60s wave of Caribbean immigration to London. The school where I worked was in a part of London with a huge influx of immigrants into an old white working-class area. The housing of these families was pretty appalling. Often families were literally living in one room, with a sink and cooker on the landing outside. I did not know Owen's exact circumstances, though I visited many of my pupils' families at home, but very probably he and his siblings slept in the same room as his parents. Children in this situation are exposed to the facts of their parents' sexual lives in an unavoidable way. This may have played a part in the graphic nature of his fantasies, and in his feeling stirred up by half-understood night-time visions. However, we have to bear in mind that all children think about what is going on between the grown-ups they live with, even if this is not usually revealed in such explicit fashion. More often their play and dreams may be the arena in which these preoccupations are expressed in symbolic form.

Beginning school

Now I shall turn to a description of the everyday events of school life and attempt to locate their emotional meaning within a child's overall development. A couple of very ordinary cameos of school life will serve to introduce this theme. Because transitions are such an important element in the rhythm and stress points of school, I have chosen two events that focus attention on this theme.

The first draws together some observations of the first day at primary school for two small girls. This was a school with a nursery class, which both children had attended for a year part-time, so the building, the teachers, and the classroom they would now be in were familiar enough. Nonetheless, the excitement and anxiety engendered by the notion of "big school" was palpable in each family. Suzie was a bright and sociable little girl. She had been much preoccupied with what to wear for her "proper school"—this was a school where a uniform was encouraged in the junior school—and this had something to do with the impressive sobriety of the junior girls' grey skirts, white blouses, and blue cardigans. Her mother's more relaxed tastes had been overruled, and Suzie looked a different child from her usual self in her grey skirt and blue jumper. In her skirt pocket, however, was a precious bit of ribbon that usually adorned her favourite teddy but was taken with her as reassurance when she was worried about something. She arrived boldly, saying goodbye confidently to her mother and little brother at the school door. The reception class teacher had suggested to parents that lunch at home for the first few days might suit some children if it were possible—school dinners were a challenge that might wait a week or so. Suzie, for all her determined bounce, had opted for that, and so her mother fetched her home for lunch. Suzie emerged at 12.30 pm looking rather dazed and with very bright pink cheeks. On the way home, she did not want to talk but just held her mother's hand tightly. When they arrived, she curled up on the sofa and fell fast asleep. Her hot forehead signalled a high temperature, and she slept deeply. Her mother rang the school to explain that she would not be back for the afternoon. When Suzie woke, she was fretful and awkward; her temperature was almost down to normal, but her relentless provocation of her 2-year-old brother was very hard to deal with. However, she ate a decent supper, and after lengthy preliminaries, with stories from both parents and much prevarication, she settled to sleep.

The next day she was better and announced with determination she was going to stay for school dinner. What a strain, thought her mother. But perhaps for Suzie the new identity of being a schoolgirl could only be sustained if she were not too much aware of also being Mummy's little girl, and of her feelings about being at school while her brother spent the afternoon with Mummy. Here is a glimpse of the enormity of the effort involved in the transition to full-time school even for a child privileged to have had the continuity of nursery class and reception and the good fortune of a mother able to be at home part-time with her children. It gives pause for thought about the stressful experience of the many pre-school children in much more full-time childcare outside the home, who have faced the anxieties of separation in earlier years. Recently reported studies of the heightened stress level in under-2s in extensive group day-care adds scientific weight to these concerns.

Suzie's friend Jessica had had a very different response to this first day. She had attached herself closely to the teacher in every possible way in the classroom and to the playground assistants at play-time. Her teacher recounted that she set herself up as a sort of teacher's helper—offering to fetch and carry, explaining what other children wanted, and so on. Jessica's way of coping had been, we might surmise, to become a very big girl and to distance herself from her more uncertain little-girl feelings by identifying with the teacher who knew everything and was quite at home in this domain. She adopted a kindly and slightly superior attitude to her fellow pupils as they struggled to find their place in the new world of the reception class. Possibly—this is an untestable but plausible hypothesis—the division of labour between Jessica and Suzie contributed to Suzie's brief collapse: while Jessica was a super-schoolgirl, Suzie retreated to a more babyish state. It we put the two girls together in our minds, we get a more complete picture of the impact of the developmental task at this crucial transition in childhood—there will be a pressure to jump forward (maybe even a precocious leap, like Jessica's) and also a pull backwards, arising from the anxiety of the new situation.

Later transitions

Each new school year, with the move from one class to another, brings up some of these same issues. The big move from primary to secondary school is a moment of intense anxiety for most children, and observations similar to those I have just described could easily be replicated for that huge change. But more ordinary events in school life, like coming back from half-term, stir children up to a surprising degree. One class of 13-year-olds gave their tutor a lot of trouble following a half-term break. There had been an additional INSET (in-service training) day for staff training, making the break quite a long one. The group was noisy, with more late arrivals for registration than usual, and more general disorganization throughout the week. There was much sniggering and obviously risqué talk going on in one small group, with frequent glances at the teacher to check on the impact of their behaviour. Enough reached her ears to make it plain that the topics of conversation included her new shoes and speculations about what she and her boyfriend had been up to. Some of the cheekier children made apparently innocent enquiries about her holiday, which were quite obviously intended to fuel this buzz, and as she was aware of their intentions, she found it quite difficult to keep cool—neither to betray embarrassment at their too-solicitous concern about her private life, nor to get too sharp and defensive to protect her privacy. Another source of disturbance was much curiosity about what the teachers had done on the INSET day—what had probably been a day of hard work for staff was turned, in the minds of these young adolescents, who felt excluded from their usual territory at school, into an exciting event in which the romantic entanglements of the teachers became the focus. As in all schools, there was a little bit of staffroom scandal, on which much could be built by enterprising adolescents. Still another feature was a couple of very cross kids, dropping books, elbowing neighbours, and scowling and sneering at the teacher. One of these was a boy in foster-care who always seemed very sensitive to changes and to beginnings and endings at school. The teacher was well used to his mixture of anger, hurt, and grumpiness towards her whenever there had been a break. She had come to understand that he was particularly vulnerable to feeling that he would be forgotten during absence and that it would take time to get past his distrust and rejecting hostility. It was as if he needed to let her feel his sense of rejection—for him, a closed school meant a place where he was not wanted. The reality that his own home circumstances were unstable and rather lacking in warmth made holiday times, when other kids often had a better time than he did, especially painful for him (Kenrick, Lindsey, & Tollemache, 2006).

What these examples highlight are some very important facts about children's relationship to school. It is a place that evokes strong feelings, and the nature of these feelings is shaped by the children's personalities and their experience of life elsewhere. The teacher and other figures at school—dinner ladies, classroom assistants, the school keeper, learning mentors, and others—all become powerful and significant figures in the child's mind. Sometimes they are perceived as friendly, helpful, and understanding. At other times they can seem frightening, hostile, superior, and unapproachable. The way all these adults actually behave does, of course, provide a real basis for children's changing feelings about them, but it is crucial to realize that just as parents are often loved and hated for reasons mainly to do with what is going on inside the child's mind—the realm of the child's unconscious feelings and fantasies—so other adults on whom the child depends will evoke similarly powerful ambivalent responses (Waddell, 2002).

Home and school

School places two demands on children: they are supposed to learn things, and they are also supposed to learn how to make friends, to play, to find a way for themselves outside the family, and to adapt to the complex expectations of an institution. The long years of maturation that human beings require are provided for primarily by family and school. Child, home, and school form a crucial triangle. Home and school are the two primary places in which the pre-adolescent child lives out his emotional life and the two that will come together in some way in his mind, for good or ill. Partnership with parents is a current concern for schools, and this matches the fact that from the child's point of view the two sets of adults in authority over his or her everyday life form an essential structure. This can be a solid and creative one, with respect for the different roles and responsibilities on both parental and school sides. Where this is so, the child is fortunate.

But even a good parent–teacher relationship will be put under strain occasionally because the child's natural tendency to explore and at times exploit differences of view and divergent standards will test out the resilience of this relationship. Living with difference—whether ethnic, religious, political, cultural, or other—is no easy task, and the cultures of home and school are pretty much bound to clash to some degree.

How this triangle of relationships is dealt with by the individual child is fundamental in his or her development. A child's loyalty to home is a core element in his or her identity and tends to be independent of whether others might see much to be criticized in the home environment or might be perfectly confident of good home support for the child. We all hold on to the place where we feel we belong with tenacious and even blind certainty. For a child, one might say it is natural to be something of a fanatic about his or her family base because this is the primary source of safety. The unknown nearly always feels very frightening (Dartington, 1998). The fact that there may be problems at home does not mean that the child will necessarily want to share these with others. In the same way, a child having difficulties in class may not feel helped by others outside the classroom taking an interest in what is going wrong. The fear of betraying people to whom we feel deeply linked and on whom we feel dependent, whether parent or teacher, is a grave matter. It is a fine line to distinguish between a respect for a child's privacy and the anxiety that damaging secrets may be holding a constraining sway—for example, the secrecy that gangs of bullies or abusive families can sometimes enforce through terror.

Triangles

The child's response to depending on two adults important to him will be shaped by the picture he has in his mind of how he feels his two parents—the primary figures of mother and father—link up. This is what Freud was trying to understand when he characterized the oedipal dilemmas of the child (Freud, 1905d). His original formulation has been extended in many ways, and his ideas have been subject to much misunderstanding and crudification, but their vital root is the necessary psychological task that faces every child in acknowledging that two parents and their sexual relationship were the origin of his life. This involves becoming one of three, and moving on from the predominantly two-person mother–child world of antenatal life and early infancy. This momentous stage in a child's development involves putting up with the experience of not being included in everything, learning how to be someone watching other people's togetherness (Britton, 1998).

So here we have the triangle of mother, father, and child. This psychological structure is subject to many variations in family arrangements—for example, a same-sex parental couple, or a parent and grandparent sharing childcare—and we need to be mindful of considerable cultural variation in family structures (Urwin, 2007). Yet the earlier confrontation in the family with a three-person situation, however constituted, stands behind the child's response to the triangle of child, home, and school that I referred to earlier. All of us, not only when we are children, continue throughout life to be subject to the painful aspects of triangular relationships. Feeling jealous, left out, passed over, intrusively curious about what we are not part of, possessive, or envious are the emotions that are stirred by this constellation. Parents, children, and teachers all have to cope with such feelings. Think, for example, of the ordinary phenomenon of the child who says virtually nothing about what happens at school to parents desperate to know how things are going. In this instance, it is the parent who feels excluded from the provocatively special relationship between child and teacher hinted at by the child's silence. In the classroom, a whispering pair of children can create the same frisson for a teacher. There is a particular edge when we experience the sense of exclusion as if we are the ones in the helpless position of a small child, a generational turn-around that alerts us to another dimension of this aspect of growing up. It is not only a matter of being left out by a pair who seem to be such a cosy intimate couple. It is also that they are often felt to be in the grown-up position. The left-out person feels him/herself to be reduced to an infantile state and under pressure to escape the discomfort of this position by often rather infantile tactics of one sort or another!

Bullying

To discuss some of the psychological challenges of school life for young children, I am going to make use of the inspired drawings of children's writer and illustrator Anthony Browne, whose pictures reveal the dynamics of some very common areas of difficulty at school, including the hot topic of bullying. This phenomenon sometimes gets presented as if it is a newly discovered problem that can be dealt with and managed by school policies and similar rationalist strategies. Unfortunately this is not the case, useful as these measures are for making it clear that school authorities are aware of the matter and concerned about it. Browne's fictional but psychologically accurate representation of the relationship between bully and victim provides illumination of these dynamics in a charming form.

His well-known character Willy is a bit of a wimp (Browne, 1991). He is lonely and left out, the only one in his world who does not have a friend and sees the world as offering no place for him. He is always saying sorry for his very existence and is amazed to discover that not everything is his fault when someone else accepts responsibility for something. Then things change. Willy and his new friend/protector, Hugh, who had previously seemed one of the bullying gang, explore the world. Willy discovers he can read and Hugh can't but likes to be read to. Furthermore, Hugh is frightened of spiders and Willy isn't. Their friendship is cemented in this equality—each can be scared stiff and each can help the other. This delightful story reveals two important facts: first, victims attribute to their persecutors much more power and hostility than they often have or feel. Second, bullies are frightened too and love to dispose of their fears by inculcating terror in their victims. When Hugh stands up for Willy, the bullies melt away. Hence the basic dynamics of the bully–victim relationship are revealed all too clearly. No doubt Anthony Browne hoped that his book will help the Willys of this world to emerge from their prison of misperception, but it is often a powerful and vicious spiral that sustains the collusive relationship between bully and scapegoat.

Clinical example: a response to staff changes

Change at school can be a big challenge, and this recurs in later childhood. A clinical example taken from the psychotherapy of a 9-year-old girl soon after the start of the new school term illustrates this. It happened that there had been many changes of staff in the school over the summer, including a new head teacher. The session, which preceded a weekend, began with the child boasting about exciting weekend plans in such a way as to place her therapist very much out in the cold. But after this the girl became very burdened, sitting at the table busily constructing complex lists of attendances, class registers, important-looking certificates relating to the head teacher's office, etc. She referred to this as her "paperwork", and it was clear that she now felt herself to be an adult with very heavy responsibilities. Her therapist suggested that she might perhaps feel that all these new people around at school really did not know much about the place or the children, and that she felt she had to fill the gap and take on the task of organizing things at school in case they were not at all up to the job. There was further exploration from this starting point of the problem of whether there was a difference between children and adults, whether children could expect to be looked after or had to do it themselves. The child explained that she was providing a "paperwork service" and explained that this meant "doing everyone's paperwork". This was the service her company provided.

Of course, there is an eloquent comment here on a child's awareness of the excessive paperwork of the modern school, but the larger point that struck me was the way in which insecurity in the context of many changes in the set-up at school had pushed this child into an omnipotent identification with the adult tasks, which, of course, would function to interfere with her being helped by the actual adults, whether therapist or teacher, since they were being displaced. Towards the end of the session, the awareness of her disturbance about new children in the class and evidence of other children's use of the therapy room surfaced—the painful jealousy evoked by this was perhaps part of what was avoided by running the "paperwork company". Important for my theme, however, is the evidence of a very bright child's profound reaction to loss,

change, and uncertainty in the school context and to the mobiliza-
tion of defences which will tend to make learning a very difficult
thing—the belief she is holding to is that she is the one who knows
and who has to take charge.

Adolescence

In the later years of school life, new horizons impinge, sometimes
with startling suddenness. The changes ushered in by puberty
reverberate through the years of secondary school, perhaps particularly and painfully evident for the 12- to 14-year-old age group
(Waddell, 2005). As the age of puberty has lowered, so the timescale during which the developmental tasks of adolescence loom
large has expanded. Earlier puberty combines with the pressures of
a mobile, image-conscious and marketized society to create strong
tensions and anxieties for young adolescents. In later adolescence,
we have a large number of young people in an extended adolescent
phase of life, still dependent on family and State as they continue
their learning in the 16–19 period and beyond into further and
higher education. This group is sexually mature but economically
a long way from independence. How they fare is much influenced
by the negotiation of the earlier stages of adolescence—the building of a sense of individual personal identity which can be differentiated from one's family of origin, the exploration of sexual
identity, the location of oneself in the social sphere—all of which
must take place alongside considerable educational pressure. The
intensity of adolescent experiences can hardly be overstated.

Clinical example: an adolescent refugee at school

Recently I was doing some work with a 15-year-old boy who came
to London as a refugee from former Yugoslavia. I heard a good
deal about his problems at school. These included all the difficulties of the many pupils in London who have to learn English on
arrival at school, and the inevitable sense of being an outsider in
numerous ways. But the most important aspect of our work was

trying to understand what interfered with his being able to think *at all*. Anything that touched off memories of the traumatic events of the war, his family's escape and harrowing journey, or their ambivalent welcome in England caused a mental shut-down of major proportions. He would go absolutely blank. For example, travelling around London remained a nightmare because of the way the crowded tubes tended to evoke his horrific journey across Europe, and he would then get into such a panic that he would not be able to plan a journey that in reality might be pretty simple. I found that, when I tried to understand all this, I felt impelled to provide active input (e.g., suggesting on one occasion different ways of travelling to the clinic), which meant that instead of attending to my job as a psychotherapist—which was to help him repair *his* capacity for thought—I would go down the track of thinking for him. This was not of help for more than a moment, however much his pained helplessness pressurized me in that direction. To tackle the fundamental difficulty, I had to put up with his mindless state, wait until we could begin to talk about the trauma and terrors that lay behind his defensive blanking out, and meantime just stick it out without denial or evasion. Although my task as his psychotherapist was very specifically to address the matter of why he could not use his intelligence to help himself, I think that some very similar issues arise in many other forms of work with young people. I strongly suspected that his teachers and social worker also sometimes tried to solve the problem of his passivity and tendency to collapse by thinking for him rather than standing by him and supporting his struggle. It was, indeed, acutely painful to be witness to his traumatized sense of helplessness.

The needs of staff

In our schools and colleges, we have many young people with serious levels of personal and educational difficulty. I want now to consider the needs of professionals in education for support in coping with the stress of their students' emotional problems. Teachers' work is enhanced by better training opportunities for relevant and restorative continuing professional development, and it is made more productive by greater investment in school buildings and learning resources to provide a good environment for their work. But in addition to that, more attention to the emotional impact of the teaching task is a vital necessity.

Opportunities for detailed discussion of work experience seem much appreciated when they are provided (Jackson, 2002; Rustin, 2008). When small discussion groups are available, teachers describe the difficulties they face with particular children, or with a specific class, or sometimes with the dynamics of staff interactions. They have the chance to gather up their reflections and impressions and to give space to the feelings these uncomfortable problems evoke. The group's attentive listening usually brings into focus some hitherto unconsidered aspect of the situation. A teacher may, to give a very simple example, realize that a particular *bête noir* in the class has the capacity to provoke as a consequence of an unnoticed personal association for the teacher. "He's got that same contemptuous curling lip as my detested older brother", one such teacher remarked with horror, but also relief at the insight, when discussing a pupil she could not stand. The support of colleagues struggling honestly with their own difficulties allows teachers to expose more of their personal reactions than they might ordinarily feel safe to, and to feel that there can be respect for the necessary confidentiality of such exploratory discussions. This sort of exploration is not a matter of people just letting their hair down, which teachers often do in the haven of their staffrooms. It is, in fact, a demanding process. The discipline of recalling and recording the troubling incidents and relationships is hard work, but this becomes much more valuable when the members of a group write an account of what they want to discuss, including as much detail as possible. Both emotional and intellectual effort is demanded from the group, but, despite this, very often the process is felt to enrich the experience of work enormously. The kind of stress that leads to burn out, early retirement, or, at a lesser level weariness, loss of creativity, or quarrelsome staffrooms and poor morale seems rooted, in part, in the immense difficulties and levels of emotional pain that significant numbers of students bring into the school and with which the staff must cope. Ways of managing the stress that are based on avoidance of the emotional impact damage the students' capacity to make use of the staff, and also damage the sense of professional competence, enjoyment, and self-worth of the staff.

Conclusion

The theoretical underpinning of this chapter hinges on some crucial concepts, which I now want to summarize.

The school is an institution designed to provide a context for the social, cognitive, and moral development of its pupils. It takes on this task on behalf of the community. The work of the school is, in fact, being progressively expanded to provide for a good deal more than schools traditionally thought was their business. *Every Child Matters* (DfES, 2004)—the official document produced after the tragic death of Victoria Climbié to outline the government's response to the failure of child protection—described the expectation that a wide range of people have to work together to achieve best practice in protecting children from abuse and that schools are seen as front-line contributors to this. We now have "extended schools" as part of community provision, and *Care Matters* (DfES, 2006a)— the White Paper that laid the basis for new legislation about children in statutory care—emphasized the role of the school. But even without all these broader aims, school is the primary work-place and centre of social life for all 5- to 16-year-olds, though the large numbers of truants and excluded pupils attest to worrying levels of failure. But in principle, school joins with the family to look after and nurture the child, with its special focus on the development of the child's mind. Helping a child to use his or her mind and body, to explore their potential, to discover the nature of the world through all the specific subjects studied at school, and to expand the child's interests in and capacities for physical, intellectual, and artistic endeavours is what school is about.

However, creating the conditions for learning is not easy. There is an important distinction to be made between learning at an imitative or rote level, which has a superficial character and does not lead to the growth of the mind (though it may fill a mind with some useful facts that can then be combined with a capacity for interpreting facts meaningfully) and learning at a deeper level, which requires personal engagement from the learner. For this to happen, something that changes the child's way of seeing things has to actually take place between the learner and the object of study. The relationship to teachers is vital in enabling such experiences of learning to take place.

How does it work? The central view I am outlining is that the child's relationship to the adult who supports learning can provide some containment for his or her anxieties about this task. This requires the adult to know what the child feels faced with—namely, the difficulties of learning (the mixture of hope and despair, of exhilaration and depression, of energy and passivity, etc.) and, through his or her greater experience of life, to be able to tolerate the time that growing up and learning requires. Dumbledore, the head of the fictional Hogwarts school, is an excellent example of just this. He could not save Harry Potter from going through things, but he was felt to be reliably concerned for him and to be properly aware of how very hard it was to grow up and to face internal and external realities.

The containment of the developmental process that schools provide is a shared task. The physical space, the security within it (not always easy to safeguard), the sense of a home-base in one's class, the ordered shape of the curriculum, the governance of the school and reliability of its rules—all these contribute something important. But most important of all is the child's sense of being recognized as an individual, of being thought about seriously over the long term with realistic acknowledgement of strengths and of weaknesses, and of the weaknesses being something for which help can be expected. This means the adults having to take on the emotional work of staying close to the children's feelings. It is entirely possible to run a school in a way that tries to ignore the emotional life within its walls, or to repress and control it in ways intended to narrow the relationship to the children's minds to a cognitive level and deal with them in more instrumental fashion. But the education provided will be thinned down for the pupils who can cope with such a regime; for those who need more help, the outcome is likely to be poor. A learner needs a teacher who can identify with the terrors and struggles of learning as well as its pleasures, not one who reduces the whole process to something more mechanized.

The complexity of the learning process means that schools are undertaking difficult, demanding, but also rewarding work. The increasing pressures on children, young people, and families in modern global society—greater mobility, uncertainty, individualization, and also opportunity—enter into the life of the school and are sources of strain for staff. But none of this takes away from the fact that teaching and learning are two of the most interesting things we can do in life, and that schools can be some of the most creative institutions we have. In a recent report on a group of students about to enter university from families with no prior contact with higher education, the common element in the students' reflections was the account of the way they had felt they were thought about by their teachers, held in mind over the long term. This is what they believed enabled them to develop, and I think they were very likely to be right. This means that the support of teachers and educational institutions has to be at the heart of effective community mental health planning and provision.

CHAPTER TWO

The school as a secure base

Nupur Dhingra Paiva

C hildren's experiences at primary school are formative and can nurture or mar future perceptions of self-worth and identity. Educational settings can be made into useful sites for working towards psychological well-being, but because schools are not themselves context-free, it is important to think about how to do so. Inner-city London schools are melting-pots of difference, and this can be threatening or become potential sources of comfort for the families linked to these schools. Practitioners working in such settings need to be conscious that it is their responsibility to think systemically and encourage the school to go beyond diversity, towards understanding the cultural struggles that may underlie children's behaviour.

This chapter highlights the emotional predicament of South Asian immigrant families and the place of emotion work in schools, especially the use of the school as a "secure base" (Bowlby, 1988) for children and disrupted families from where to explore. The clinical work described in the chapter took place in inner-city London primary schools and is presented as an example of how it can be beneficial to use this secure base for further growth.

"A secure base" is the phrase John Bowlby (1988) used to describe a central feature of parenting: a base from which a child or adolescent "can make sorties into the outside world and to which he can return knowing for sure that he will be welcomed when he gets there. . . . In essence, this role is one of being available, ready to respond when called upon to encourage and perhaps assist, but to intervene actively only when necessary" (p. 11). Other authors have extended the metaphor by including the family (Byng-Hall, 1995) and community (Papadopoulos, 1998) as secure bases. I suggest, in a similar vein, the use of the school as a secure base for immigrant families, as a place from where they can gain the confidence to interact with other, less nurturing institutions. With many schools in the United Kingdom now working towards becoming "extended schools",[1] the idea of using a school as a focal point for the community and for psychological well-being is not new or farfetched.

Immigrant parents frequently complain that their children, born in the family's country of adoption, do not listen to them. In the educational/clinical setting described in this chapter, parents of children aged between 5 and 11 years who had been identified by school staff because of their poor social adjustment and fluctuating educational achievement described violent temper tantrums at home and outright disobedience towards them, yet compliance at school. The broad identifiable pattern was of quiet, withdrawn young girls and aggressive, inattentive young boys.

Behavioural techniques and parent training programmes such as the Incredible Years Parent Training Programme (Webster-Stratton & Mostyn, 1992) and the Triple P system (Positive Parenting Program: Bor, Sanders, & Markie-Dadds, 2002) are frequently used in these situations to help parents manage their children's behaviour. However, depending on the complexities in the family, these interventions have been known to not have lasting positive effects (Webster-Stratton & Reid, 2003). Akhtar (1999) writes that "A poignant confluence of cultural, generational and intrapsychic conflicts characterizes such scenarios" (Akhtar, 1999), and the work involves disentangling the difficult communicational knots. Group-run behaviour-change-focused parent training programmes based on social learning theory are often not successful with immigrant families or non-white populations. Differences in cultural goals of childrearing are difficult to explore or even acknowledge in a group setting, and disentangling communication knots requires a more in-depth approach (see Paiva, 2005).

School-based group work with young girls provided some insight into their struggles. Some were concerned with age-appropriate questions of changing bodies; others expressed their struggles around moving between two schools (their mainstream school and an evening faith school); the treatment they received in comparison to male siblings; and the lack of intergenerational communication. Many said that they loved school and did not like holidays because they had to stay home. Further assessment revealed that these children were surrounded by unclear boundaries—of race, language, rules, of their place in the family, and of attachment figures. Complex family dynamics of unresolved losses, denial, and secrets contributed to the fragility of boundaries. Most had little belief in firm safety nets at home that could contain their anger, fear, or rebellion. Parents were experienced as weak and ineffective. As a result, the children repeatedly challenged them, yearning for them to be stronger.

This chapter seeks to understand these fragile boundaries by knitting together the emotional contexts of South Asian immigrant families; their children's inner battles to belong to someone or some place; incomplete statutory sector mental health provision for a multi-ethnic population; and the place of emotion work in schools, especially how it may be used as a secure base to explore children's integration to a different culture. The aim is to encourage practitioners to include an understanding of race, colonization, and culture so as to take children's systemic experiences seriously, since these are essential to psychological well-being.

The chapter uses psychodynamic, systemic, and some postcolonial concepts as a theoretical base, despite the three not always being compatible. It is written from a perspective of ownership, since I am also an immigrant from a South Asian country to the United Kingdom and was introduced to life in London through two educational institutions—the institution I joined for further clinical training, and the inner-city London primary school where I had my first part-time job as a learning support assistant. I have found that the emotional themes in the clinical work frequently resonate with my personal experience.

The emotional predicament
of South Asian immigrant families

One might imagine that most South Asian immigrants to the United Kingdom suffer because they lack facility with the English language and therefore miss out on information, which reduces their access to resources. However, this could be considered as the overt symptom of a much deeper and complex affliction of cumulative disempowerment. In an attempt to be truly psychosocial, I use a postcolonial and systemic approach to illustrate how the real contexts of history, politics, and socioeconomic differences create present-day emotional contexts for these communities.

Figure 2.1 (Paiva, 2005), informed by Complex Systems theory, illustrates the multiple systems making up the identity of a South Asian immigrant to the United Kingdom. The diagram indicates the non-linear, irreducible, dynamic nature of these different areas of experience and helps us to consider the multiple layers of emotion that an individual has to negotiate in daily life. I use Erikson's (1956) views on identity as a starting point. He discusses psychosocial identity development in young people in great depth and gives options as to what the term "identity" connotes. He explains that identity development includes "two kinds of time: a develop-

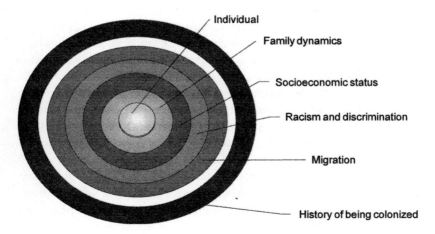

Figure 2.1   Multiple systems making up the identity of an immigrant.

mental stage in the life of the individual, and a period in history" (Erikson, 1968, p. 309). In addition it has a "complementarity of past and future both in the individual and in society". In this chapter, I use the term *identity* to mean "a conscious sense of individual identity" as well as the "maintenance of an inner solidarity with the group's ideals and identity" (Erikson, 1956, p. 102)—a continuity between themselves and some of the world around them (Erikson, 1968, p. 296).

The contribution that each context/layer in Figure 2.1 makes to the identity of South Asian immigrant children in the United Kingdom is elaborated below.

The history of being colonized is a context that influences every South Asian immigrant to the United Kingdom. Colonialism continues to provide a social frame for the lives of hitherto colonized communities, and a postcolonial understanding pushes us to consider that knowledge construction is political and that assumptions about the "other" were made from the viewpoint (or "gaze") of the powerful colonizer. The colonizer's attitude—that they are the superior being, with greater ability, knowledge, capacity for moral judgement, and intellectual resources, and the corollary that the colonized are inherently racially inferior—is often internalized, by both colonizer and colonized. Repetitive physical brutality, economic exploitation, and valuing the masculine over the feminine reinforces the view that the colonized are only useful as a physical resource and are otherwise effeminate, childish, sub-rational, and psychologically weak and therefore need a master. Some authors (e.g., Shengold, 1989) call this "soul murder" and consider this historical/ political context an important reason for disempowerment.

However loose we may consider the influence to be, it forms part of the context into which the next generation is born. It leads to self-doubt, not only about personal areas of knowledge but often about cultural identity. This is not restricted to unskilled or semi-skilled workers or to people with low literacy, but also applies to professionals who deal with a more hybrid colonized identity (see Nandy, 1983). Their interaction with local institutions, social services, and health and professional bodies, as well as their interactions on the street, often only work to reinforce this sense of disempowerment or anger. For the purposes of therapeutic work (in this case, through clinical psychology), it is important to consider the client's and professional's perceptions of the distribution of power, resources, and knowledge between them and the other. The clinician, regardless of cultural background, needs to consider the power differential between him/herself and the client—children and adults alike. How do the clients perceive the clinician—as a representative of the majority culture, or as a member of their community? How do these perceptions change which issues can be discussed between them?

Migration means leaving behind familiar places, things, people, relationships, foods, sounds, and expectations. In addition to these losses, migrants move to a place where there may be no one with a "background" on them; they arrive as a blank slate for others to project onto (see Akhtar, 1999). This is especially true for the women of a traditional South Asian family, for whom stringent social hierarchical structures also provide a network for emotional and child-rearing support. In the absence of such a network, mental health difficulties borne out of isolation, disconnection, and a lack of positive experiences are common. Transcontinental arranged marriages and "chain migration" (www.migrationwatchuk.org) ensure that in every family, there is often one adult facing this struggle afresh.

The increasing threat to religious identity is a significant factor in disempowering the common, non-fundamentalist follower of Islam—again, mainly women and children. Fears of being looked at, approached, or attacked on the street are no longer elements of paranoia but are a response to what is projected onto them in the present milieu in the United Kingdom.

All of this has direct impact on the individual's perception of his or her role and effectiveness as a parent. In addition, ethnic-minority parents feel that the State and schools undermine their parental authority by implying that they are better parents to their children. The majority of South Asian immigrant families (Maitra, 2006) and African families (Joseph Rowntree Foundation, 1997) see State involvement as implying inadequate parenting, an attitude that they resent, and they are afraid that their children may be removed into State care.

Children born in the country of adoption tie their immigrant parents to the new land:

From the moment of their birth . . . in general, parenting ne-
cessitates a greater familiarity with the local culture. Food
eaten by the family begins to change. . . . The story books read
to children inevitably contain a large share of those drawn
from local reservoirs. Homogenizing television shows and local music begin to populate the family's transitional space. . . .
If the children's local origin and behavioural style are experienced as threatening, an ethnocultural tug of war begins at
home. Empathy for other family members suffers. Dialogue
between parents and children gets derailed and the cultural
difference instead of enriching the relationship, fuels a hateful
strife between generations. [Akhtar, 1999, p. 26, citing Mehta,
1997]

It is into this complex emotional system that the individual child
is born. Alongside a child's temperament (Thomas & Chess, 1977),
which is substantially determined by his or her genetic blueprint,
parental expectations and wishes affect the way in which a new-
born is psychologically "held" (Winnicott, 1965) by the mother's
attention. For an environment to hold a child effectively, both
family and culture need to provide containment, especially of ag-
gression (Akhtar, 1999, p. 88). For immigrant South Asians, this
complex system often creates a space where family myths and
secrets, conflicting wishes, and intergenerational transmission of
traumatic events or a sense of cumulative ineffectiveness influence
the child's future identity formation. In this emotional context,
fragile boundaries around a sense of personal continuation and
confused solidarity due to a lack of clarity concerning what defines
the group are not surprising.

The children's inner battles to belong

In one of my first interactions in this new work context, acutely
aware of my own immigrant status, I naively asked an 8-year-old
British-born Bangladeshi girl the question, "where are you from?"
She responded, very clearly and with no qualms, "I am from
here". Her response made me wonder if I had needed to ask a
clearer question about where she felt she "belonged". Akhtar (1999,

p. 104), an immigrant himself, writes that immigrants have an eternal longing to belong that is never quite fulfilled. To me, the child's response underlined the gap between how second-generation immigrants perceive themselves and how they may be seen from the outside—by mainstream society and by their parents. I imagined that as she got older, her answer to my question might begin to get more complex.

Erikson (1968, p. 303) writes that "Every person's psychosocial identity contains a hierarchy of positive and negative elements, the latter resulting from the fact that throughout his childhood the growing human is being presented with evil prototypes as well as with ideal ones", For the South Asian immigrant, Akhtar (1999, p. 80) describes the split clearly: an east-to-west immigrant often develops ideas that Western culture is characterized by greed, sexual promiscuity, violence, and disregard of generational boundaries, whereas Eastern culture is seen as a place of contentment, instinctual restraint, love, humility, and respect for the young and the old. For the immigrant, this provides a convenient, ready-made split of object representations. The second generation has to encounter this split on a daily basis but with different values attached to the two parts.

Erikson's theory helps me to understand these children's inner battles to belong; the youth of an oppressed and exploited minority, who "is aware of the dominant cultural ideals but prevented from emulating them, is apt to fuse the negative images held up to him by the dominant majority with the negative identity cultivated in his own group" (Erikson, 1968, p. 303). Prevented from being part of the white majority and unable to believe that there are positive elements from within their own cultural community that are worth emulating leads to inferiority feelings, and self-hate is therefore common among South Asian youth.

My formulation was that on a day-to-day level, many of these children were struggling with feeling un-"held" by their families, who represented their cultural community to them. Some were clear that they experienced their parents as ineffective—as disciplinarians, as the people in charge, or as communicators. One young girl's mother said that her daughter would get onto her back and say "I want to see if you are stronger than I am". Another was anxious, felt unprotected, and described fears such as being at-tacked on the street. Given the cumulative disempowerment their parents may be facing, this is not surprising. In addition to dealing with pre-adolescent questions of identity, these children were also in the process of negotiating a pluralistic integration. They had yet to figure out which aspects of their culture of origin to retain and where to accommodate changes.

The school as a secure base

Mental health professionals who are skilled at working with clients across cultures make us aware that it is important to help them dis-engage cultural differences from intra-psychic conflicts, since the two frequently overlap. Intra-psychic difficulties can make cultural differences appear more problematic.

School could provide the necessary holding environment where such children feel kept in mind. The challenge for the clinician is to navigate through the mistrust that exists between home and school.[2] Schools often consider themselves as being better parents to the children than are their parents. The parents often feel that their authority is undermined by the "all-knowing" teachers. Ne-gotiating this involves clarifying whose purpose the clinician is being recruited for when a referral is presented: whose agent are you being invited to become? In other words, whose problem is it? The child's? The parent's? Or the school's? It is an important aspect of the work to involve parents at every stage: in getting consent, explaining the process of psychotherapy and the possibility of dif-ficulties increasing before they diminish, and making them aware of what changes to look out for.

Despite the challenges, there are some clear advantages to using the school as a base. Being seen as part of the school system and provision makes it simpler to involve parents at the different stages of intervention as well as to get consent. For the children, it normal-izes the experience of being worked with individually. It becomes a privilege to be taken out of class and have individual attention. The attention is often therapeutic in itself. For parents, there is no extra burden of attending appointments at a different location, usually associated with medical concerns or "madness" (any phrase with the word "mental" in it brings up this fear). Since it takes place within school hours, this aspect of it is invaluable and has far more chances of getting the parents' cooperation. Since parents collect their children from school, it becomes possible to have informal conversations with them prior to any formal meetings.

Another advantage of primary-school-based work is the possibility of setting up groups to work on specific issues with children. This approach can be used to enhance social skills, confidence, and positive interactions with peers and creates the possibility of joint projects for parents and children to be involved in. For example, one inner-city primary school I worked with had an English as a Second Language (ESOL) project for parent's of 5- to 6-year-olds. Once a week, these parents came into school and had an English lesson given by a qualified ESOL teacher. After this, they spent an hour with their 5-year-olds in the classroom. The school found that it increased parent–staff interaction and communication, gave immigrant parents an understanding of the school experience of their British-born children, and helped their acquisition of the English language.

Simple interventions of this kind illustrate that some of the emotional difficulties these children face can be prevented and addressed by providing them and their parents with experiences that they can share. It can form the starting point to bridge the cultural divide in which they live. When immigrant parents say that their children do not listen to them or that they have difficulties with them, it goes beyond behaviour. It reflects a complex convergence of cultural, generational, and intra-psychic conflicts. The difficulties, therefore, are for the therapist working with them. Disentangling such communicational knots is never easy, but it is a crucial aspect of working with these families.

Below is an illustration of these ideas and struggles using school-based therapeutic work with a young girl, whom I will call Henna.

Henna

Henna was a 9-year-old second-generation Bangladeshi girl who was referred for therapeutic intervention by school staff after she expressed a desire to throw herself off a bridge during a school trip.

School records showed that Henna was the middle child of three children. Henna's family had been referred to the local child & adolescent mental health service (CAMHS) three times. They were offered an appointment on at least one occasion which they did not attend. On another occasion, a mental health practitioner made a home visit for an assessment. Unfortunately, the professional making the visit was a white, English-speaking, male member of the CAMH team who visited without an interpreter. As expected, he found he could not work with the family in those circumstances and left. There was no follow-up.

The school had also referred Henna's family to a local family-support unit, and a Bangladeshi lady visited them weekly. She described the family as isolated within the community and uncommunicative and that she found it difficult to get them to interact with each other as a family.

Henna's school records also had some information on her early childhood: her mother had reported that she had not held Henna when she was born and had not formed a bond with her; she also considered her to be different from the other children because she would not come forward for comfort if she was hurt or ill. After meeting the school staff and her parents, I understood that Henna behaved very differently at home and at school. (Her mother did not speak any English or Urdu, so we had the assistance of an interpreter. Her father spoke Urdu, and our conversations took place in this language.) In her father's opinion, she was just being a child—lively and childish—though he admitted that she was difficult to manage. He reported that he was nearly 70 years of age, suffered from diabetes, and had a lot of responsibilities being the father of three children. He described his wife as being ill, ineffective in her mothering, and not the same since she had lost her first-born child more than ten years ago.

It was clear that there were some difficulties in the attachment bond between Henna and her mother. From the father's report, it appeared that mother was dealing with unresolved grief about the loss of her child. Henna, born soon after, was very much a replacement child and unfortunately of the wrong gender, born to a depressed, grieving mother. For her mother, the trauma was worsened by the fact that Henna looked like her brother. The mother had also given her the female version of his name. (See Abraham, 1911, for a discussion on this phenomenon.)[3]

Henna's mother was convinced that there was something wrong with Henna's brain and thought her "mad" at times. She gave a few examples: at home one afternoon, Henna had decided to take her brother's school uniform and stick it down the toilet. At mealtimes, if she didn't like the food, she would simply fling her plate onto the floor or spit food out.

When I met Henna, she came across as a quietly confident child. Through play she showed me that she wanted to be the only child to her parents. However, her greater concern was that her hatred and anger would damage people beyond repair. From the start, she chose paint as her mode of communication to express this, and she was prolific with it. She produced up to three different paintings in a 50-minute session. Her first paintings were similar: they were of different colours, clearly separated from each other by strict boundaries, exceedingly controlled and neat. After a few sessions of this, we agreed that colours were feelings and that for her it was safe to keep feelings all separate and away from each other. However, at the same time she verbally expressed a desire to throw paint all over the room and make a mess. Because our early conversation on boundaries had specified that we cleaned up at the end, when I reiterated the rule and reminded her of our ground rules, Henna decided against the paint-throwing. This made me wonder if Henna was asking for a firm boundary that could stand up to a challenge, one side effect of which would be that she would feel safer expressing her justified anger.

Reiterating the rules to Henna proved to be a turning point. From this point on, the paint on her sheet began going over the edge and onto the table. At the end of every session she would insist on cleaning it up, by herself. In fact, the cleaning, or repairing the damage, became more elaborate and exciting than the painting. We managed to clarify to each other that it was okay to make a mess, because no damage was done; it could be cleaned up too.

This idea made her eyes shine, and she insisted on repeating it for weeks. She then decided she was going to tell her mother the same thing.

In her final painting, Henna allowed paint to blend. I like to think that by then it was safer for her feelings to be allowed to flow and come together—to be thought about and expressed. The coming together no longer led to a mess, and Henna may have had some positive experiences, learning that it could always be cleaned up.

Discussion

Therapeutic work with Henna or her parents would not have been possible had the intervention not been in the school setting. The school's failed attempts to get the family to be seen by the local CAMH service was a classic example of South Asian immigrant families being disempowered. Their needs were "invisible" to the mainstream, who did not consider it important to take their cultural and language needs into account.

The school setting made it possible to meet the parents, gain their consent, and invite them to discuss their concerns about their daughter's behaviour at home. Henna's mother found our conversations useful and attended regularly. She also provided feedback about Henna's behavioural changes. When the intervention ended, Henna's mother expressed an interest in learning English and started attending ESOL classes at the school.

Henna's behaviour appeared to be a result of feeling un-held by loose boundaries. She managed to use the boundaries of the therapeutic setting to her advantage and extrapolated them to her relationship with her mother. The difficulties in this family were cultural, intergenerational, as well as intra-psychic, and I believe that behavioural intervention—even in Bengali—would not have touched on these complexities. This school-based intervention was a minor one; however, it may have created opportunities for Henna and her mother to build a positive bond, which is crucial for healthy development. As many authors note, "Predominance of love is the glue of the unified representation" (Settlage, 1991, p. 352).

Conclusion

The school is the obvious place to situate any prevention- or early therapeutic intervention-oriented service since it takes advantage of the existing boundaries, which is a fundamental but often missing element in the lives of immigrant children. These structures provide reliability and predictability to young children and can also be useful for their families when introduced with a user-friendly attitude and with cultural sensitivity.

Notes

I am deeply grateful to Sadegh Nashat and the late Professor Phil Richardson for their encouragement and supervision which made this work possible.

1. Extended schools provide wrap-around childcare from 8 am to 6 pm along with many activities for the children and parents attending the school. These activities can include sport, music, fitness, study times, play, parenting skills training, information for support from social services and housing, childcare, computer training, English for Speakers of Other Languages, math, etc. (see www.direct.gov.uk/en/parents/childcare/index.htm).

2. Projects placing mental health professionals in primary schools were piloted in inner-city areas and frequently came upon challenges around engaging parents (DCSF, 2008b).

3. A child conceived soon after the loss of a significant person in the mother's life might become unconsciously equated in the parental psyche with the deceased when there is unresolved grief in the mother. "The psyche of a replacement child is the recipient not only of the mother's expectable wishes but also for the deposited representations of the mother's earlier love object. . . . These acquire a realistic shape often encoded in the first name the child is given" (Abraham, 1911, pp. 31–32).

CHAPTER THREE

Integrating reintegration: the role of child & adolescent mental health professionals in supporting the inclusion of excluded pupils

Mike Solomon

This chapter considers the role of CAMH professionals in promoting the reintegration of excluded pupils into mainstream education in inner-city settings in the United Kingdom. This involves more than just direct clinical work, as there is much more scope for intervening at wider systemic, organizational, and inter-agency levels. This includes a consultation role, both within exclusion settings and across the boundaries between mainstream and exclusion settings. I argue that, by offering containment and a different perspective on crossing organizational boundaries and opening systems, mental health professionals working within education can help to promote the reintegration and inclusion of vulnerable children and young people in mainstream settings.

I outline the practice and experience of reintegration, using examples where different mental health contributions have supported pupils' reintegration. I will then begin the discussion with an outline of the unconscious factors underlying exclusion. The mental health role is then conceptualized using frameworks from psychoanalytic, systems theory, and group relations literature. These are all used to propose that CAMH professionals in exclusion settings can take up a "third position" in relation to reintegration, offering a consultative role to promote the reintegration of excluded pupils. I then argue that this role has the potential to transform a series of dyadic relationships—within the family, school, and education systems—into a series of triangular relationships, offering the possibility of taking different perspectives and creating a space in which projections of anxiety may be contained, thus promoting the conditions in which reintegration and inclusion are more likely to succeed.

Definitions and contexts

I use the term "exclusion settings" to describe any segregated education setting into which pupils have been placed because of their behavioural difficulties. The mainstream education system has judged that pupils' behaviour has warranted them to be excluded, temporarily or permanently. Exclusion settings in the United Kingdom may be separate units within mainstream schools, or separate services altogether, such as Pupil Referral Units (PRUs), that are alternatives to mainstream placements. Reintegration is the process by which pupils are re-included in the mainstream system, whether or not it is the same school setting from which they were originally excluded.

While not all pupils will have their needs best met within mainstream education, there is a significant group of pupils who, having been excluded from mainstream settings, can be supported to return to mainstream education. This relies both on the pupil and the setting being prepared for such reintegration and on mainstream settings being supported to "keep their doors open".

CAMH professionals include psychologists, systemic and psychoanalytic psychotherapists, and occasionally others (such as psychiatrists or nurses) who may be based in a CAMH service or clinic. It is becoming increasingly recognized that CAMH professionals can make a key contribution by not just working alongside education professionals, but actually by being based within education provisions for dedicated amounts of time. Their role in education is likely to include responding to referrals for assessment and intervention regarding particular pupils—individually or in groups—but may also include staff training and consultation work with education colleagues.

So, in what ways can mental health professionals make a difference in exclusion settings and help to promote reintegration? One way of thinking about this contribution is in terms of the different levels of intervention that mental health professionals can offer, including:

▹ working individually with pupils, offering assessments and/or psychological therapy
▹ working with parents and carers, or with whole families
▹ working with both home/families and exclusion settings
▹ working with both exclusion and mainstream settings
▹ working with both education and other agencies.

Four examples of different contributions are now described.

Examples of the mental health role contributing to reintegration

Case example 1
David and "the prison" : "reintegration-in-the-mind"
in a mainstream secondary school

Even without an immediate prospect of reintegration, the presence of mental health involvement in exclusion settings implies the possibility of change and so introduces the idea that this is something that can be thought about.

While working for a limited time in a mainstream secondary school in Inner London, I liaised formally with the Deputy Head Teacher, who coordinated referrals that school staff could make for mental health input. However, as referrals were slow in coming, I visited the school's internal exclusion centre. This was a separate building within the school site, which was kept separate by a high fence and a locked gate that could only be unlocked by the staff working within it. Pupils were not allowed to mix with those on the other side of the fence, had separate break times, and had lunch brought to them to eat inside the building. Not surprisingly, it was known throughout the school as "the prison".

When I "dropped in", the staff inside "the prison" seemed surprised and pleased to welcome me, and they talked about how they felt separate from the rest of the school. They mentioned one pupil in particular, who had been asking to talk to someone about his worries. Although this was a self-referral rather than one passed through the Deputy Head Teacher, I agreed to see him.

David was a 15-year-old boy who had been internally excluded for aggressive and violent behaviour. It seemed that the school were very close to excluding him permanently. The Deputy Head Teacher appeared quite reluctant at first to agree to me seeing him, as if the school had "given up" on him.

David himself was worried about a forthcoming court appearance. He talked to me about his past experiences with guns and knives, and how he was currently trying to turn things around. He was finding this difficult because of his context as a member of a local gang and the ongoing stress of the legal process. David used our conversations to think about his dilemmas, and while there was no clear resolution by the time I had to leave the school, David himself still had a place at school.

The impact of my work with David appeared to be felt at different levels.

For David himself, I was an adult who tried to help him to think about his situation and dilemmas. The school staff in the "prison" were sympathetic to him, but they felt they had reached the limits of their time and expertise in supporting him. David seemed able to use his sessions with me to think differently about his situation and choices, making use of the opportunity to have some space to think and reflect (Winnicott, 1971) and to consider thinking as an alternative to action (Bion, 1962b; Klein, 1946).

For the school staff within the "prison", my presence and curiosity seemed to help them feel valued and appreciated. The "prison" boundary appeared to surround the staff as well as their students. They felt separate from the rest of the school and that they were regarded differently by those in authority. They felt that they were the ones who were sympathetic to troubled students, while the rest of the school wanted those students controlled and managed, "out of the way" in the "prison". They viewed my time with them as a valuable resource, and my appreciation of their welcome seemed to mirror their appreciation of my input and interest in their work.

For the Deputy Head Teacher and the wider school system, my time working in "the prison" seemed to force their eyes to be opened. David and other excluded "inmates" were no longer quite as "out of sight and out of mind" as they might have been. The wish to exclude them from the organizational mind, to "give up on them", had, I think, been challenged by the incorporation of an outside mental health professional whose involvement implied the possibility of understanding, change, and "conversion" (Roberts, 1994). It seemed that the school's experience of having its internal boundaries crossed helped to offer an alternative to the defensive mechanisms of splitting and projection (Bion, 1959, 1962b; Klein, 1946). "The widespread use of splitting as a defence . . . can be particularly entrenched between different levels of an organisation. . . . However, when staff can take time to think about needs, demands and difficulties relating to the task, instead of feeling ignored, resentful and powerless they feel more in touch with their expertise" (Foster & Roberts, 1998b, p. 222). It is possible to see my intervention with David in systemic terms as one way of creating a space for mutual curiosity across the internal boundaries in the school, which prompted understanding as an alternative to the projective processes in play within the school system (Foster & Roberts, 1998b; Klein, 1959).

Case example 2
Anna: consultation and containment within
an exclusion setting

Mental health professionals can offer a valuable contribution by thinking with staff in exclusion settings. One means by which containment can be offered is with regular consultation meetings with staff in Pupil Referral Units, where pupils are educated after permanent exclusions from mainstream UK schools, and from where they may be reintegrated.

In one discussion of Anna, a 13-year-old girl who was due to return to mainstream school from a PRU, staff in the unit spent a lot of time talking about Anna's preoccupation with asking about whom she would be supported by on her return to school. Her mentor in the unit also worked in the mainstream school for part of the week. However, she said that she had told Anna that "there's another mentor in the school". I responded by saying how easy it might be to underestimate the importance of the attachments that pupils had formed to particular members of staff during their time in the unit. It seemed that there was a tendency to avoid, or at least minimize, the reality of the importance of those attachments, and the responsibilities that went with them, by depersonalization ("there's another mentor in the school"). This was one of the institutional defences against the anxiety of dependence found by Isabel Menzies Lyth (1959) in her seminal study of the nursing profession.

The discussion turned to thinking about the importance of pupils' attachments to staff during their time in the unit, and about what it might be like for pupils to be returning to mainstream school. The staff group became more able to think about reintegration as a "lived experience", rather than as a depersonalized procedure. The group also became more able to think about what might be needed to manage that process successfully, in terms of the external and internal worlds of the pupils. In this way, the mentors became more able to think of themselves as transitional objects (Winnicott, 1965), secure and reliable attachment figures needed to support pupils to cross the organizational boundaries on returning to school.

This example shows how exclusion-setting staff themselves can be supported to think about the experience of reintegration for pupils, schools, and staff. The containment offered by the consultative frame (Bion, 1962b), providing a time and space in which staff could "play" with different ideas (Winnicott, 1971), helped to overcome the social defences against anxiety (Menzies Lyth, 1959) and to promote thinking across the organizational boundaries.

Case example 3
Peter: consultation across education boundaries

Peter was a 13-year-old boy who had been permanently excluded from mainstream school for being found with a knife in school. Until that time he had been involved in some fighting and bullying, but nothing that had carried particularly serious consequences. On arrival at the PRU, his father asked for psychological support for Peter, and so I met with Peter initially for a psychological assessment. It emerged that Peter lacked confidence in himself, and had been bullied by peers in his previous school. He joined bullies as a way of protecting himself from becoming a victim. Peter seemed to lack some social skills in expressing himself, and he and his father agreed that they would like this to be the focus of some individual therapeutic work. Peter made generally good progress in the unit, and a mainstream school was approached and agreed to offer Peter a place.

Peter also made generally good progress on his reintegration. However, this was not smooth or consistent, and there were a number of "hiccups" when Peter was involved in incidents of disruptive behaviour. I arranged to meet with his Head of Year and mentor in the new school and offered some guidelines on ways of working with Peter. I also recommended that school staff met regularly with Peter and his father to try to help contain Peter's anxieties and to maximize the chances of consistency across home and school. This seemed to be a new idea, as I think that education colleagues would have worked mainly with Peter himself individually. By offering a formulation that involved thinking about the family, integrating what was understood at home, at the unit, and at school, he was helped to feel more contained in making a "new start". Peter made excellent progress in school, and he returned to the unit two years after leaving, to let staff know how successful he had been in taking public examinations and that he planned to continue his studies into further education.

This example illustrates the value in working across educational boundaries, in making the education system more open by combining the shared expertise of the family, the exclusion setting, and the mainstream school. The contribution of a containing presence crossing boundaries between educational systems helped to promote thinking about Peter in ways that were readily accessible and available.

In their book about school exclusion, Sue Rendall and Morag Stuart highlight the importance of schools remaining open systems to help vulnerable pupils:

> When families and/or schools are "open" systems, in that they engage in a continuous exchange with the environment . . . there is likely to be an acknowledgement and awareness of the difference, and of the potential for tension and conflict. Teachers and parents in "open" systems will be more able to help pupils to think about the expectations of the different systems and to contain anxieties which may arise. Members who make up systems . . . bring their "outside school" experiences into the school context. [Rendall & Stuart, 2005, pp. 178–179]

The contribution of a CAMH professional sharing understanding and providing containment across boundaries in an open system can greatly help the chances of pupils like Peter maintaining a placement in mainstream education.

Case example 4
Sonia: consultation across agency boundaries

Sonia was a 13-year-old girl on the verge of being permanently excluded from her mainstream secondary school. The school made a referral to a specialist behavioural unit for an 8-week intervention programme. This was presented as "one last chance" before a permanent exclusion.

I was asked by the school to work with Sonia. Her mother found it difficult to attend, and Sonia agreed to meet me on her own. She was reluctant to "talk" but was able to tell me about her practical strategies for managing her anger. She told me she and her mother had recently moved home, away from other young people with whom she used to get into trouble. She told me that she was making different choices now about her friendships and peer group and was successfully avoiding getting into trouble.

Sonia's school wanted her to see a psychotherapist in school, as a "condition" of her returning to school. Sonia made it clear that she did not want to do this. I thought that there was a potential for creating a split between Sonia (and her family) and the school (and the psychotherapist). Consequently I met with the therapist and the Deputy Head, to discuss different perspectives on support-ing a successful reintegration. I then joined the psychotherapist in meeting with Sonia and her mother, as a review of Sonia's progress on her return to school rather than as a precursor to "therapy". In this way, a space was created for talking about Sonia's progress, for reinforcing the school's responsiveness and growing flexibility, and for co-creating alternative ideas about what might be helpful. This resulted in a shared agreement that it would be helpful to have regular reviews of Sonia's progress that included the school's psychotherapist, rather than frequent "therapy" sessions that Sonia would have felt to be punitive. Subsequently, Sonia successfully stayed on at school and then took up work experience training in beauty treatment.

This work with excluded pupils illustrates the value in being able to reformulate situations by offering alternative perspectives on "problems" and "strategies and solutions", particularly in at-tending to, and supporting, the voice of the child. Rendall and Stu-art (2005, p. 181) report that excluded pupils and their families feel powerless and impotent, and that any staff who may support them tend to carry little influence. A CAMH professional can potentially carry significant influence. By exploring the different perspectives in Sonia's case, and by giving equal weight to all parties, it became possible to influence those in positions of power and reach a plan agreeable to all.

This is perhaps a good example of how systemic approaches can be helpful in reducing school exclusion and promoting inte-gration:

> Systemically, the importance of interactions in different contexts is relevant in the home–school context. . . . Circular question-ing, picking up on themes which emerge from the individual perspectives of the family or school members, identifying di-lemmas and providing each member with equal status and power in working together to resolve dilemmas might be help-ful. [Rendall & Stuart, 2005, p. 177]

A conceptual framework

This discussion begins with an outline of what may be the unconscious influences on "exclusion settings" within mainstream society and education, and their implications. Different frameworks are then used to conceptualize the contribution that mental health professionals can make in reintegration.

Exclusion settings and the unconscious desires that they fulfil

There are many conscious reasons to exclude pupils whose behaviour is disruptive and challenging. However, there are also unconscious motivations to exclude—or evacuate—disturbance, distress, and misery, which mainstream schools, and society in general, would rather not have to see or think about.

These motivations can be thought of as societal defences against anxiety, as collective unconscious wishes for disturbance and distress to be split off and projected into excluded pupils and the settings that work with them.

There is a societal wish to "turn a blind eye" to the needs of vulnerable and challenging children. The realities of such children and their life experiences can be felt to pose too great a "danger" and to be too painful to face and think about. This means that there is constantly a danger of these excluded pupils—and the exclusion settings where they attend—becoming what Angela Foster and Vega Roberts would describe as "asylums for our own projections" (Foster & Roberts, 1998a, p. 37), just like long-stay mental health institutions.

When faced with such situations, "we seem to have to avoid drawing the unhappy conclusions which a realistic appraisal would demand. We can only carry on our lives as normal by turning a blind eye" (Steiner, 1985, p. 169). Without reintegration, segregation can serve to contribute to the creation of "the other", defined by Paul Hoggett as "a container for that which I cannot bear, for that which the individual or collective body lacks the capacity to understand as a part of itself" (Hoggett, 2000,

p. 60). This can be applied both to excluded pupils and their families, and to the exclusion settings that work with them. Often those children, young people, and families who are most in need have been those who were seen to "not engage" with clinic-based mental health services. The introduction of CAMH professionals into the education system can be regarded as one way in which mental health services have "opened their eyes" to previously invisible client groups.

Implications for the task(s) of exclusion settings

If these unconscious desires are acted out, without check, then there are likely to be significant implications for individual pupils and staff, as well as for the wider system. There will be pressure for exclusion settings to be "closed systems", with barriers preventing exchange with the external environment, rather than "open systems" in which people, information, and ideas may be exchanged across boundaries (Reed & Palmer, 1972).

Paul Hoggett describes "bad sense" as "concrete thoughts, hard and unmalleable. They cannot be used for thinking. They do not represent anything" (1992, p. 88). In this paranoid-schizoid state, it is as if thought is a noun, a thing, rather than an action or experience to be explored. Isolated, concrete thoughts replace an open, fluid process of thinking as linking and making connections (Bion, 1959; Klein, 1946). "Bad sense" offers solace from the persecutory anxieties of thinking about reality. The implications for PRUs, internal exclusion rooms, and other exclusion settings are clear: if they become closed systems, then they will simply become refuges, a solace from the painful and persecutory anxieties involved in thinking about the needs of vulnerable school pupils (e.g., "the prison" in Case example 1). If they only offer the concrete "holding", they will concretely represent the "bad sense" involved in such retreats from the painful realities of those young people who are most vulnerable in our society.

There are dangers that excluded settings themselves might come to mirror their pupils, so that they themselves become excluded and segregated from mainstream schools and services. The

UK charity Barnardo's (Cooper, 2001) found evidence that schools, units, and other services that work with children and young people with social, emotional, and behavioural difficulties can find themselves isolated. Staff themselves can come to feel marginalized and separate, and boundaries between organizations might only rarely be crossed.

Within mainstream settings, staff working in designated behavioural and/or learning support services may become identified with their pupils, and they may even themselves become "challenging" within school systems, representing a different perspective for thinking about the needs of challenging pupils (staff in "the prison" in Case example 1). In more specialized exclusion settings, staff may feel even more separate and marginalized, especially if they have little or no contact with mainstream education.

The implication of this danger (of exclusion settings becoming "closed systems", where nothing comes out, and little or no change is possible) is that the primary task of excluded settings would be simply to "hold" such disturbance—holding in a concrete, rather than psychoanalytic, way—to avoid "contamination" with mainstream education and mainstream society.

This can mean that exclusion settings may become holding places comprised only of bricks and mortar, offering only concrete holding. There is a pull towards exclusion settings themselves becoming more separated and isolated, cast adrift from mainstream society, as if they were long-stay institutions or prisons. This means that exclusion settings must have to work extremely hard to counter the tendency to become the destination at the end of a cul-de-sac, one-way streets with little or no prospect of a return to mainstream education for pupils who have been excluded. They are expected to provide concrete holding of "the other", based on "bad sense", so fulfilling a wish to split off painful realities for the rest of mainstream society. They perform this task on behalf of the rest of us.

That out of sight is out of mind
Is true of most we leave behind.

[Arthur Hugh Clough, *Songs in Absence*, c.1860]

Widening perspectives in the reintegration process

So how might reintegration be conceptualized, given such a context of segregation? Within education, reintegration is often thought about solely in relation to the child. "Change" is something that happens within-the-child (sometimes within the family). The onus is on the pupil to "change", and support to do this is offered through behavioural interventions and targets work with home, parents, or carers (dependent on resources). Success then depends on the pupil's "performance".

Without the involvement of professionals from other agencies, changes are only likely to happen within an education context. The relationships in the excluded settings will still be dyadic—namely, between pupil and teacher, between family and school, and also between exclusion and mainstream setting. Psychoanalytically, this can be thought of as a "pre-oedipal" constellation of one-to-one relationships, with little "space" to explore different perspectives or to "play" with different ideas of difficulties, solutions, strengths, and change. It may be hard to move beyond familiar perspectives and patterns of relationships.

However, given the unconscious pressures towards exclusion, it would seem that reintegrating excluded pupils back into mainstream education is a process and a task that must overcome unconscious resistance at different levels.

Reintegration implies the possibility of a "two-way journey", rather than a cul-de-sac. OFSTED (2007), the UK's education inspectorate, have recently highlighted that a key factor for success in PRUs is staff conveying to pupils that these units offer a "second chance" or a "fresh start". The implication is that there is the possibility of understanding, through assessment and formulation, and that there has been some kind of change—in either the pupil or the environment, or in both—that means that integration is now possible (see Case examples 3 and 4).

In terms of open systems theory (Miller & Rice, 1967; Roberts, 1994), the exclusion setting becomes an "open system", having taken in, or "imported", an excluded pupil, done something to make a change (or "conversion"), and then "exported" a pupil ready to be reintegrated into a mainstream school that is prepared to include him or her. The process of "export"—of preparing a mainstream setting for re-inclusion—can be as important as the "conversion" process within the child or family. A previously excluded pupil becomes "visible" again to the eyes of the mainstream, and pupil and school alike are supported to prepare for inclusion (see all case examples).

In the case of Peter in Case example 3, by meeting in the mainstream school with the Head of Year, by giving a written set of strategies, and by recommending regular meetings with Peter's father, it was as if I was providing the school with an extra "set of tools" that they could use practically to support Peter's reintegration. In the case of Sonia in Case example 4, it was by relaying and amplifying Sonia's articulate voice that I could help to influence the school that they need not "use every tool" at their disposal. The value of formulating a plan that included the voice of the pupil (Sonia) and family (mother)—while including a "bottom line" for the school—was that it made the reintegration more likely to succeed.

The contribution(s) of the mental health professional

The role of a mental health professional in exclusion settings can be conceptualized in this context as contributing to the widening of perspectives regarding reintegration. This is particularly valuable when the provision is regularly and reliably accessible within exclusion settings themselves, when mental health professionals can straddle organizational boundaries, contain anxiety, and help exclusion settings and their adjoining systems to become even more open, as illustrated in the case examples above.

Taking up a "third position"

By virtue of being a non-education professional within an education setting, a mental health professional can take up a "third position" that is different from pupils/families and different from schools, teachers, and other education staff. This can enable different kinds of conversations to happen in schools (Dowling & Osborne, 1994), creating a triad around a symbolic "triangular space" in which new thinking and new patterns of relationships may be created. For example, it becomes possible to think about patterns of relationships in terms of authority through having access to a third party who is neither pupil nor teacher. Also, planning the reintegration of pupils into mainstream settings may be made easier if anxieties around mental health or behaviour issues are contained by the involvement of a mental health professional, particularly one who straddles boundaries themselves (Case examples 2, 3, and 4).

A "triangular" reflective space can be created by a mental health professional taking up a "third position". This involves holding on to uncertainty and not knowing, and to curiosity and ambivalence, while reflecting on the interactions and relationships between pupils and staff, home and school, and helping staff to reflect on their own roles in relation to their pupils (such as Anna in Case example 2). In such ways, a staff team can be helped to "think about itself while being itself" (Britton, 1989, p. 87). The perspective of a CAMH professional from such a "third position" can also help pupils and schools to look at the relationship between them, by being curious and relaying both the wishes and concerns of each to the other. In the case of Sonia (Case example 4), this helped to create a more successfully negotiated reintegration plan than would otherwise have been the case.

Promoting "depressive-position" functioning through containment

Mental health professionals can play an important part in facilitating shifts towards more depressive-position thinking—both within exclusion settings and across the "gap" between specialist and mainstream settings. They can offer a containing space in which thinking can develop that links with the painful reality of pupils' experiences, rather than concrete "bad sense" predominating. The "depressive position" is characterized by being able to stay in touch with reality, including experiences and emotions that are painful. It is an integrated state of mind in which thinking is possible, as opposed to the "paranoid-schizoid position", in which painful experiences and feelings may be split off and got rid of through unconscious projective processes (Klein, 1946). Importantly in this context, the depressive position is never attained permanently but is always a state of mind that requires work, containment, and repeated experience to reach.

Mental health professionals can help to facilitate such depressive-position thinking systemically by providing arenas in which new ways of understanding pupils' behaviours, states of mind, and needs can be thought about and shared. The containment potentially offered by a mental health professional is, according to Bion (1962b), the unconscious process by which experience is felt, processed, and then fed back in a more digested form, which can then be integrated, thought about, and learnt from. This is most effective when combined with the containment provided by strong management, together offering "containing leadership that involves the creation of a relational and mental space that helps in the toleration of ambiguity, uncertainty and anxiety" (Simpson & French, 2005, p. 294). By providing contained and containing spaces for thinking, mental health professionals can help to address and contain anxieties of education staff and, by so doing, can lead to increased understanding of, and empathy for, vulnerable young people. When containment is provided across organizational boundaries, pupils become more visible in the eyes of mainstream staff and institutions, and the "split-off" parts that they represent can begin to be mentally "re-integrated", as illustrated in all the case examples above.

The presence of a CAMH professional crossing the boundary between exclusion and mainstream setting, sharing an understanding of emotional and behavioural needs in general and of the re-integrating pupil in particular (e.g., Peter, Sonia), can go a long way to containing some of the fears and anxieties of the mainstream school. Previously excluded pupils can begin to be understood, their needs met, and their voices valued, rather than them simply being seen as "other". By crossing the boundary between exclusion and mainstream setting, the contribution of a CAMH professional can both contribute to and represent this shift, accompanying re-integrating pupils in their journey from the margins back into mainstream. The CAMH professional's role in exclusion settings, therefore, can be viewed as one of containment, offering the possibility of understanding, support, and transformation, with an explicit aim of maximizing the opportunities for inclusion and reintegration into the mainstream.

Promoting multi-agency working

Traditionally, reintegration has been promoted by teachers and other education professionals largely alone. While they clearly still need to take the lead, vulnerable and challenging children have a variety of substantial needs, which are unlikely to be met solely by education professionals. OFSTED has confirmed that in the United Kingdom "few Pupil Referral Units have the staffing or expertise to meet the very severe needs of some pupils with behavioural difficulties" (OFSTED, 2003, p. 10).

More recently still, OFSTED has highlighted the importance and value of partnership working for supporting excluded pupils (OFSTED, 2007, p. 5). The integrated presence of a CAMH professional can help to strengthen the exclusion setting as an "open system"—not just an open education system, but open to imports and exports across service and agency boundaries. CAMH professionals can make a key contribution in promoting the integration of PRUs and other alternative education provision into a whole system of support for young people—an aim of the UK Government in the White Paper *Back on Track* (DCSF, 2008a).

This role can be particularly valuable when education professionals and systems are under pressure. In times of pressure and threat, different perspectives may not be welcomed or encouraged, and there may be a pull towards undifferentiated opinions and judgements. "In groups under threat, the unconscious pressures on members to blur differences can be enormous—as if safety lies only in oneness" (Mosse & Roberts, 1994, p. 152). This can be the case within exclusion settings, and also across exclusion and mainstream education. The value of having a containing reflective space to think about different perspectives may promote different ways of thinking about pupils, including new ways of thinking about their needs for successful reintegration and how these might be best met, as outlined in the case examples above.

Conclusion

Direct clinical work is only part of the story of the contribution made by mental health professionals in exclusion settings in education. The case examples and discussion above illustrate the value of integrating mental health provision within exclusion settings in education. This can be understood in terms of opening the boundaries between mainstream and exclusion systems, by providing a "third position" from which different perspectives can be observed and reflected upon. This enables anxieties to be contained better and allows the painful reality of vulnerable and challenging pupils to be thought about and responded to carefully, rather than simply re-enacted in education settings.

By offering containment, mental health professionals can help pupils, families, and colleagues to feel less excluded and more "held-in-mind" across organizational boundaries. By transforming a series of dyads into triadic relationships, mental health professionals within exclusion settings can create thinking spaces in which projections of anxiety can be contained and so can contribute to improving the chances and the experience of inclusion and reintegration. They can help to promote the possibility of "reintegration-in-the-mind"—for young people and their families, for exclusion settings and their staff, and for mainstream schools and society.

CHAPTER FOUR

The Mediation Model: a conflict resolution approach for the promotion of the psychological well-being of children and adolescents

Joseph Rieforth

In this chapter, I concentrate on the concept of "systemic mediation", which is based on the notion of a conflict as positive. A conflict can be a crucial opportunity in students' social education, and mediation as a communicative technique can be helpful in creating new contexts for learning in organizational structures.

I also outline the systemic approach in mediation, the systemic concepts and goals used, and the model, which is based on central presuppositions such as flow balance, interdependency, and the idea of human behaviour being a reaction to internal and external context conditions.

Furthermore, I describe the principles of problems and their solutions from a systemic point of view, including the introduction of the Nine-Field Model, a model that uses different levels of strategic questioning.

For mediators in schools, coping with pupils and teachers in a mediation process requires various skills, as the situation is usually highly emotional. The danger of getting personally involved in the conflict should not be underestimated. Besides general interpersonal competence, the mediator also needs skills in counselling, in order to develop a professional relationship with all parties involved. To relate those competences to the organization "school", I will give a brief outline of essential elements of organizations, including schools, from a systemic perspective.

Mediation: definition and history

Mediation is a structured method for a constructive resolution of a conflict, one in which both parties—with the help of a third party—seek an amicable solution serving their needs and interests. In a conflict, both parties usually insist on their gridlocked positions. Any deviation from their own position would be considered a defeat, and the enforcement of their own position is usually interpreted as a victory. In such a situation, conciliation often becomes difficult. In the context of mediation, it becomes essential to find a solution that all conflict parties involved work out for themselves, that they comprehend and are able to accept. In contrast to judicial disputes, all parties involved have the opportunity to influence the decision at any time.

In overview, there are three fields of activity that can be considered for mediation:

1. *Family mediation*—particularly in the area of break up and divorce, but also increasingly in the context of intergenerational and heritage conflicts.
2. *Economic mediation*—particularly for conflicts within an organization (within a department, leadership–employees, board of directors–workers committee, etc.) or between businesses (e.g., company–company subsidiary, holding company–affiliated company).
3. *Mediation in the public sphere*—particularly in the context of public construction (roads, buildings, waste deposits, energy questions such as wind energy, railways, and airports).

In considering the development of mediation and its relevance in the different fields of activity (family, economic, public sector), one can develop different perspectives. In terms of a "social justice story", mediation is a bottom-up instrument of liberation and social organization that citizens can use to take their conflicts into their own hands and, in so doing, can create justice. In contrast, the perspective as an "oppression story" emphasizes the use of mediation as an instrument for pacification and oppression: by means of tactical negotiation/conversation and a fixed structure, mediation calms the underprivileged and fleeces them. Both views are extreme and have been put into perspective over the course of time. Today, mediation is mostly viewed as a "satisfaction story". According to this view, mediation is considered an effective and satisfactory way of resolving problems and comprises only a minor degree of political consciousness. For the sake of completeness, the perspective of viewing mediation as a "transformation story" will be mentioned. This view is not so much about problem resolution in a particular case but, rather, about permanent solutions through personal growth, thus leading to a change in the whole organization or society (cf. Baruch Bush & Folger, 1994).

The systemic approach in mediation

The cornerstones of a successful mediation are similar to those in other counselling settings—that is, building up a trusting atmosphere through the participation of a neutral third party. The latter's task is to develop, within a given structure, the framework for the parties involved to participate actively in the conflict resolution. Apart from presenting special codes of practice and a predetermined scheme (which cannot be dealt with in more detail here—for more information, see Ballreich & Glasl, 2007; Glasl, 1994, 1998), the mediator guides both parties through this process with the help of conversation techniques based on a development-oriented attitude for the handling of counselling and therapy processes. It is essential to consider the conflict dimension, the willingness to reflect one's own role in the conflict, and the building up of understanding for the other conflict party and to identify desires, aims, and interests for the basis of adequate solutions. Therefore, "impartiality" and neutrality—in the sense that the mediator does not prescribe a solution as a communicative attitude—are of utmost importance to a successful settlement of the dispute. A main characteristic of success in mediation is a self-determined development of solutions by the parties involved in the conflict.

Systemic concepts

The systemic model as the basis for the mediation process creates an appropriate foundation for the provision for all persons involved, for the different starting points, and for the strengthening of resources (cf. Bamberger, 2001; Stierlin, 2001; Von Schlippe & Schweitzer, 1996).

As an overview, the following propositions can be highlighted:

1. Every individual is part of a greater whole—that is, in mediation it is significant to know the important others behind each conflict party (e.g., in family mediation, the parental couple; in business mediation, the representatives of the board or the employee committee as representatives of the employees; in the public sphere, the residents or people affected, who are represented by advocates in politics or administration).

2. Systems organize themselves according to given patterns and rules—that is, it is not the individual him/herself that is the focus of attention but the patterns and rules of communication between the individuals. Knowing the communication structures is a prerequisite for conflict resolution.

3. Every individual develops his or her own inner landscape, particularly in the conflict resolution process, where one has to make transparent what the respective situation means to the parties involved—the issue is not that of an objective reality but of finding out the subjectively constructed reality of the conflict parties, which is the foundation for the solution of the conflict.

4. The action of the individual is the action of the other (mobile dynamics)—the importance of viewing social situations as a circular chain of cause and effect is one of the decisive findings of systemic theory. In the context of conflict resolution, this presents a further level for processing.

5. The process of watching changes involves being watched (the story of the counsellor)—the meaning of the person in the role as mediator is crucial to the conflict resolution process. The mediator's own attitudes, experiences, and courses of action in conflict situations provide the space for creative recreation of the conflict history. That is why self-reflection of one's personal history is so important for the mediator.

6. Social systems cannot be briefed in a direct way, but they can be stimulated by new information relevant for the system—the mediation model presupposes that the solution can only be developed by the parties involved themselves. The systemic model supports this process further by presupposing that any kind of external influence (mediator) will only be taken into consideration by the conflict parties if they consider it reasonable.

Systemic goals

Systemic mediation as a solution-oriented method for conflict situations follows some basic objectives:

1. *Stimulation of change*—this is based on the idea that new, external suggestions (information) stimulate a social system to evaluate patterns and rules anew and, if necessary, change attitudes or behaviour in certain situations.

2. *Development of greater independence (individuation) and exchange with other social systems (relatedness)*—the strengthening of individuality by becoming aware of one's own needs and interests while at the same time facilitating the ability to maintain relations to others form the basis for a growing conflict competence.

3. *Increasing options for actions*—expanding courses of action as a resource for handling conflicts is a basic goal of systemic action.

The systemic model

Like any model of human interaction, the systemic model is based on some central presuppositions, such as the idea of a permanent willingness to change in social systems (flow balance), the idea of mutual influence on the individual system members (interdependency), and the idea that all human behaviour is a reaction to internal and external context conditions, which also makes sense to outsiders if the decisive rules and patterns are detected.

Accordingly, systemic counselling/mediation constitutes a growth- and development-oriented idea of man. It is oriented towards resources and simultaneously includes an appraisal of problems and conflicts and the idea that each instance of problematic behaviour is based on a positive intention.

Systemic intervention

Systemic intervention is conducted in several steps. During the whole process, respectful curiosity and appreciation for the clients is the focus of attention. The quality of the relationship with the mediator thereby improves and ensures permission for different kinds of intervention. These interventions can then be of a "disturbing character" for the clients in order to dissolve deadlocked patterns of communication and behaviour. What is crucial to the use of these interventions—usually in the form of questions—is the permanent appreciation of the autonomy of the client. Accepting the goals of the client means support for developing the resources available.

The process of mediation is always used in conflict situations in which a rather large number of different people are involved. If one considers the conflict parties involved as independent social systems, it becomes clear that all people involved experience the current situation as problematic. This "experienced" problem and its consequences for the conflict resolution process are considered in detail below to reveal the intra-psychic and interpersonal dynamics and to point out the advantages of the Nine-Field Model (Kuhlmann & Rieforth, 2004, 2006).

The basics of a problem from a systemic view

What makes a problem a problem? In general, a situation is experienced as problematic if the following conditions apply:

1. at least one person subjectively experiences the situation as problematic;

2. one person has a wish or need for a change to the situation;

3. it is currently impossible for one person to generate a solution for the situation.

Hence, it follows that the problem that is experienced and the possible solution are interwoven and that the wish to change presupposes the problem. At the same time, this means that the person who experiences the problem knows the wish to change and therefore also the solution to the problem. The person having the problem thus is the expert in finding the solution. The mediator is needed for the process of problem-solving, not for finding the solution to the problem.

These conditions account for some of the assumptions made for the practice of counselling and mediation, which ascribe an explicit role to the mediator. The role of the mediator is that of accompanying the process of problem-solving and supporting the mediants in developing solutions. To arrive at the solution, it is mainly the mediator's communicative skills that are needed here. In the context of the mediation process, the mediator has to stimulate the problem-resolution skills of the mediants, which already exist, and to induce new courses of action. If the conflict parties become aware of their own resources, and new conflict resolution competences are generated, this provides the mediants with the energy necessary to arrive at the solution. One of the fundamental skills of the mediator is the art of asking questions in this context. Besides the assumption that each experienced problem is based on a "hidden wish", the questioning technique is a special opportunity for comprehending the situation by addressing different levels by questions:

▷ Questions asked on the level of the *problem* provide the mediator with differentiated feedback about how the mediants experience the problem.

▷ Questions asked on the level of the *solution* provide the mediator with important feedback concerning the "hidden wish or desire", in the sense of individual interests and needs.

▷ Questions asked on the level of *resources* provide the mediator with crucial feedback in regard to which skills and opportunities for problem-solving the mediant ascribes to him/herself and to which kind of changes he or she is ready for on his or her own initiative.

Strategic questions on all levels of the Nine-Field Model

This strategic technique of questioning manifests itself in the Nine-Field Model. The selection of questions is oriented towards the model. The first three levels of the model can be imagined like this:

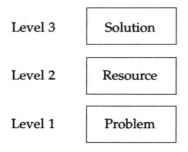

Level 3	Solution
Level 2	Resource
Level 1	Problem

This method allows the mediants to become aware of their inner "experiencing" of the conflict situation. Awareness of at which level the mediant is operating (diagnostic aspect) makes it possible to use questions strategically for change towards a problem solution (interventional aspect). The decision about which question addresses the respective level adequately depends on the mediator's communicative skills and process competences.

Expanding the model:
introducing the temporal dimension

So far we have described three levels of the model—problem, resource, and solution—which provide orientation and intervention in the conversation. Let us now expand the number of levels to include the temporal: past, present, and future. In this way we arrive at the two-dimensional matrix of the Nine-Field Model. This matrix is the "working field", so to speak, or the "questioning field", for the process of mediation. Combining the process-steered questions with the temporal dimension, the matrix shown in Figure 4.1 develops. Summing up, one can say that the mediation process takes place in the following sequence:

1. It is essential to build up relations. In order to do so, the mediator should provide an introduction by means of open questions and create a comfortable working atmosphere. The mediator has to establish a framework for cooperation and commitment to mediation/counselling. Furthermore, she or he must clarify the expectations of the conflict parties involved. In doing so, the *systemic attitude* has to be characterized by appraisal—that is, the steps undertaken previously to solve the conflict must

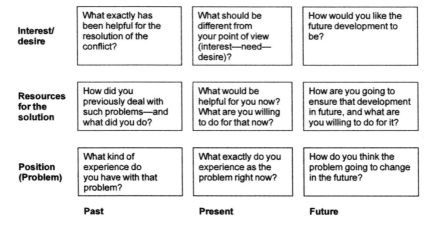

	Past	Present	Future
Interest/ desire	What exactly has been helpful for the resolution of the conflict?	What should be different from your point of view (interest—need—desire)?	How would you like the future development to be?
Resources for the solution	How did you previously deal with such problems—and what did you do?	What would be helpful for you now? What are you willing to do for that now?	How are you going to ensure that development in future, and what are you willing to do for it?
Position (Problem)	What kind of experience do you have with that problem?	What exactly do you experience as the problem right now?	How do you think the problem going to change in the future?

Figure 4.1.   The Nine-Field Model (Kuhlmann & Rieforth, 2004).

be recognized. Moreover, it must also be characterized by respectful curiosity and transparency, which helps to prevent fears. Finally, the mediator should develop hypotheses and thus increase the perspectives of solutions.

2. The mediator has to substantiate the concern. To do this, the mediator has to identify the history of the conflict and the positions of the parties involved and collect the topics of the dispute in order to define an agenda as a common space for processing. Concerning the systemic attitude, the mediator has to demonstrate "impartiality" by means of temporary partiality. In other words, she or he has to take the position of each party involved for a certain time in order to understand their positions. On the whole, however, the mediator has to remain neutral and to respect the boundaries of the system. She or he has to lead the conflict parties into taking responsibility for their own positions and has to create an atmosphere of hope (empathy) for the successful resolution of the conflict.

3. The mediator has to find a common level for processing all interests. To move from problem to solution, the *holistic corporal force* of the *wish-vision* has to be considered (Nine-Field Model). Furthermore, the *systemic attitude* has to be characterized by respectful curiosity. It must develop creativity and desires, be based on an appreciative strategy, and convey pleasure in being supportive.

4. The mediator has to provide a stimulus for solution. Therefore, it is necessary to initiate change, develop ideas, find common variants, and make decisions for solutions. Hence, it is essential that the *systemic attitude* is marked by appreciative moderation, demonstrates pleasure in development, cooperation, and self-independence, and is resource-oriented.

5. It is the mediator's responsibility to develop agreements. The mediator should therefore summarize the process, name the most important system changes (new patterns and rules), say good-bye to the mediants, and thank them for their cooperation. A *systemic attitude* characterized by impartiality, appreciation, strategic guidance, cooperation, and gratitude are vital conditions for a successful end to the mediation process.

Competences of mediators in the school

Mediators have to possess quite a number of skills, as it is necessary to get the parties involved in a highly emotional situation in
order to concentrate on themselves and on the other party. Thus
a mediator needs to have not only a general interpersonal competence, but also special counselling competence. The biggest challenge of a mediation process for the mediator is to not get involved
in the conflict and, at the same time, to build up a professional
relationship with all the parties. The individual resolution of the
conflict regarding the content demands a highly professional counselling competence, as can be found in other counselling settings
as well. This includes the art of asking questions, active listening,
reframing, goal orientation, moderation, visualization techniques,
and so forth. For topics prone to conflict, a basic knowledge about
conflict dynamics and different meanings of conflict types, coupled
with an assessment of the course of the conflict as well as some sort
of field competence and system knowledge about the process of
ascribing meaning to the situation experienced as problematic, are
indispensable. In addition, the awareness of the mediator of his or
her own reactions and personal behaviour in conflicts is of great
importance for his or her competences. Unfortunately, this sort of
self-awareness or self-reflection has so far been neglected in the
quality debate for the training of mediators.

Personal skills and systemic objectives in a school class

As already pointed out, a social conflict is not only based on different points of view, but at least one person has to complain about
the inappropriate behaviour or view on things. If a rapid understanding of the behaviour experienced as conflictual takes place, or
even some kind of compensation occurs such as asking someone's
forgiveness, the conflict is usually settled spontaneously. The decision about which behaviour or which rules and patterns of relationship are considered legitimate or illegitimate in a given system
depends on the respective system members. The permanent conflict latency present and its disruption potential in social systems
can be reduced if these rules can be articulated and communicated.

That is why, in a class in a school, the transparency of existing rules and the articulation of subjective opinions of all system members involved is a basic prerequisite for the development of a mediation culture and is also an important objective.

Every student should be able to express his or her subjective view on the legitimate and illegitimate claims, norms, and violation of norms in the context of cooperation in class. Because of the common transparency in class, these will finally be considered as universally valid, and adherence to them can be demanded and expected from everyone.

The self-developed norms are then reflected upon in a permanent process. This always takes place in a slightly modified form, because they are not static rules but social feedback of continuous reciprocal action between the system members (students/teachers) in a joint learning process. Hence, another important objective is to renegotiate the relativity of the agreed rules and norms in the current discourse. Students get to know normative dilemmas this way and develop their own scepticism about simple normative truths, including their own perceptions. The art of coming to acceptable results in spite of this only "relative accuracy of agreements" increases the competence in class for manoeuvrability and furthers mutual appreciation in the learning process. The more students are involved in this process by teachers who are trained in mediation, the better the chances that the insight gained in the current conflict can be used for further "social contracts" in life. Experience has proved the introduction of a "class council" to be of value. In this forum, norms and rules of cooperation can be defined in a ritualized form and contracts about the forms of social behaviour can be agreed upon. In a given case of conflict, one must first find out whether the parties involved in the conflict really have different normative opinions, or whether one party knows of the violation of norms but nevertheless feels to be right due to previous norm violations by the other party. In the latter case, one must reconstruct the conflict history and the reasons for the behaviour in connection with subjective normative opinions. Experience in mediation (Montada & Kals, 2007) has shown that talking about comprehensible reasons for the party affected can help to reduce indignation and thus help to de-escalate the conflict.

Furthermore, both parties being experienced as taking responsibility should be encouraged. This way one can recognize how consequences are rated (un)consciously and understood in terms of personal or property damage or threat. In the context of schools, they may concern social acceptance, the just appraisal of achievements, the just distribution of rights and duties, and solidarity within the class. All these cases present not only some form of competitive behaviour, which develops within a learning and achievement community as a positive development, but also a dysfunctional and aggression-releasing form of interference— for example, in forms of disregard, power demonstration, offensive criticism, property damage, and so forth. These situations are decisive for whether the extended forms of handling conflicts and the personal skills and competences of all those involved will lead to a recognition of the situation or whether a resolution will be avoided. The latter usually takes place if one person is too afraid to get efficient assistance from a third party or out of fear of being criticized him/herself and to be wrongly accused of complicity without the escalation of the conflict really being looked into. Again, I would like to point out here how important it is to involve the past for an appreciation of the conflict history and for detecting possibilities for the conflict resolution that have been undetected so far (cf. Kuhlmann & Rieforth, 2004), which is contrary to the advice one usually finds in the literature on the mediation model—namely, not to get involved with the past in order to create a future.

Institutional prerequisites

In order to establish mediation sustainably in an organization such as a school, one has to consider the personal competences of those involved and the modified learning processes in the respective class, as well as the basic elements of organizations. The division into several fundamental areas allows for a differentiated analysis of strengths and weaknesses in each case and hence the development of possibilities for a systemic intervention. At the same time, it prevents students and teachers committed to the mediation concept from bearing alone the responsibility for the change or for failure.

Only by involving the organization direction (school board) can the conditions for a sustainable change be created. The willingness on the institutional level is a prerequisite for reducing conflict costs in the long term, but unfortunately it is not yet sufficiently developed in many schools. This runs the risk of relocating the conflict dynamics from the school board to the level of the students, similar to the parentification of children in a family. Following the basic elements of organizations developed by Glasl (1994) for business corporations in particular, their relevance for the further development of the school as an organization is pointed out below.

Essential elements of organizations

In the following, a short overview is presented of the elements of organizations that give some stimulus for the establishment of a mediation culture (cf. Philipp & Rademacher, 2002).

▸ *Identity.* Here, the focus is on the basic values of the school as well as its historical self-image and its external image—for example, that of teachers, students, and other schools in the region. This self- and external perspective of one's own identity has to be specified.

▸ *Concepts, strategies.* This category takes into consideration the school profile, the school regulations, long-term school programmes, and guidelines for the handling of internal conflicts with students, teachers, and further cooperation partners. Questions concerning the strategy and the participants, which have to be attended to, as well as future challenges are the focus of attention here.

▸ *Structure.* The structure of the school board as well as its principles are focused upon and also the structural relation to external groups and institutions (e.g., youth welfare services, partner schools, etc.). Questions of leadership—and the experience of it as beneficial or obstructive for the introduction of change processes—are possible here, as well as the assessment of existing coordination structures.

> *People.* This category focuses on the knowledge and skills of all employees in the school—which also comprises persons who are not part of the teaching staff, such as secretaries, janitors, and so on—with their attitudes towards the organization, informal structures, and working atmosphere and the style of contact with external institutions. That is why questions about evaluating the quality of cooperation and the handling of previous conflicts come into play here, including questions related to appreciation and praise and to the structure of staff development.

> *Functions and bodies.* This category addresses duties, competences, and responsibilities of the individual in his or her respective function as well as in the respective bodies such as teacher and school conferences, commissioning and project groups, as well as institutions that are external to the school. Questions that could be developed could attend to how clear the individual functions and duties are defined—for example, which functions are of particular importance, and which functions do nobody want to take care of or are not even assigned to anyone.

> *Workflow and process.* Here the focus is on investigating the internal processes of the teaching processes (primary), team work (secondary), and conferences (tertiary) and the internal logistics and raising of third-party funds and relevant information. These questions concern the efficiency and effectiveness of these processes and the necessity for change or specification by the school board.

> *Resources.* All physical resources that can help to support the mission of the school are attended to. This includes the ecology of the building, the equipment, and the financial resources as well as the importance of the school in the region, its connections to the transport network, and the granting of funds. What standards does the school have concerning rooms and professional resources? How satisfied are the employees with the teaching resources at their disposal, and how do they evaluate the development in the coming two years? How do they classify the location of the school and its importance in the region?

The school/organization from a systemic perspective

This perspective on the school as an organization suggests a systemic analysis of the whole situation in which individual subsystems can be examined and, at the same time, the continuous interdependency can become more important.

In the traditional school model, many teachers still think that not having any conflicts in one's class is a sign of high professionalism. Inevitably, this attitude leads to a rigid separation of the class subsystem from the total school system with a fixed boundary (cf. Minuchin, 1974). The necessary discussion about helpful and obstructive influences in the class between individual teachers fails to appear. This often hinders the possible conflict between individual members of the class, because the internal boundaries in the class system are often blurred; differentiation by the teachers is not possible, and there is no perspective (Figure 4.2). Also, on the *level of the whole school as an organization*, there is often no adequate discussion between teachers. Moreover, the contact with external institutions (youth welfare services, neighbouring schools) is often limited and takes place in a limited way (Figure 4.2).

A sustainable change in the way conflicts are handled within a mediation culture can only be successful if enough time is allotted to discussion about the details of the topic. This assumes

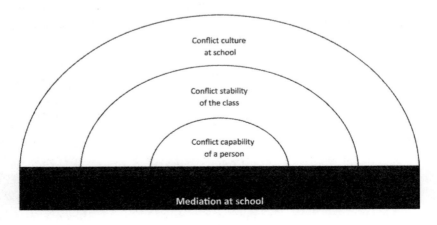

Figure 4.2

the unreserved willingness of the school board to support this process of change and not only to provide resources, but also to get actively involved in the process themselves. This developmental process requires a rethinking and the introduction of new behavioural patterns at the top of the organization. From there, they are conferred upon the teaching staff. Only once a sufficient number of colleagues have acquainted themselves with this new way of thinking will their training as conflict mediators gain significance. These new circumstances allow for disputes to take place with new patterns of behaviour when resolving conflicts in class and adhering to the rules of the total organization and protecting participants from taking responsibility one-sidedly. At the same time, a new stimulus can emanate from this foundation, which can be useful for the development of an overall strategy for a new conflict culture.

Case study

Conflict situation

In my capacity as a mediator, I had been approached by a teacher from a local integrated school. She and a colleague were class teachers of a 9th Grade (comparable to a Year 11 class in English schools). The class consisted of 30 pupils aged about 15 years.

The conflict was about the behaviour of a group of female pupils. The girls had started to keep a record of negative information about three classmates. The affected pupils felt severely bullied by this action and subsequently were not able to participate in the lessons without fear of pressure from the other girls. They ended up making more and more mistakes. Within the class, two opposite camps started to develop. One camp supported the "book of mistakes", the other backed up the affected girls but were not able to do anything about the situation.

By the time I had received the request from the class teachers, the conflict had already escalated onto the parental level. The parents accused each other of being responsible for the situation. The pressure on both teachers increased, and something had to be done to defuse the situation. The teachers' previous attempts to find a solution included private conversations and discussions within the existing class council, but none of those attempts had been helpful—on the contrary, the conflict was aggravated after some of the interventions. After preliminary talks, I suggested a combined parents' evening, with pupils, parents, and teachers, in order to find a solution to the simmering conflict.

The parents' evening took place approximately ten days after my first contact with the teachers. Right at the beginning of the meeting a pupil's father came up to me and pointed out that his son should be in bed by 9 p.m. in order to be well rested for the next school day. It turned out, however, that this pupil was well known for going to bed very late. So it was obvious that the father's comment expressed the tension and the degree of severity of the conflict.

Mediation process

After the parents and their children had taken their seats, I gave a brief round-up of my preliminary talks with the teachers and explained the structure of the current meeting. I wanted the different groups (pupils, teachers, parents) to explain the conflict from their own perspectives or talk about those topics that seemed important in this matter. For these purposes, I had arranged chairs in two circles, an inner and an outer circle. I asked the pupils to take a seat in the inner circle. Teachers and parents took their seats in the outer circle. The rule was that only those sitting in the inner circle were allowed to speak.

At this instigation, the seating arrangement was changed immediately, causing an initial "systemic pattern interference" between parents and their children, who had until then been sitting next to each other. The attention was focused on those pupils affected by the conflict directly. In the first round of talks, it turned out that the pupils were very glad to be invited to the parents' evening and appreciated that they were the first to speak.[1]

It became clear very quickly that the pupils were dissatisfied with a number of learning conditions during lessons and at school in general. Obviously this was news to both parents and teachers. The conflict between the girls faded from the spotlight. I supported this impulse and asked the girls: "What ideally do you need in order to learn?" The pupils then expressed their opinions and kept a record of the findings on presentation cards, which I had supplied beforehand. The cards were then put on a Metaplan board. After this initial collection, I asked the parents to change seats with their children. The pupils then joined their teachers on the outer circle. Ignoring the pupils' comments, I asked the parents: "As parents, what do you wish/require from school?" The parents' topics were also collected and put onto the board. After that I asked the teachers to sit in the inner circle and respond to my question: "How do you experience the current situation, and what kind of support do you need?" They collected their conclusions and put them on the board. I thanked everyone for their committed and straightforward willingness to talk about the topics that haunted them. While everyone mingled in the lobby, I sorted the collected topics and arranged them into five main topics:

Situation in school subjects	Working structure	Study location	Autonomy	Exchange

After a brief explanation of the topics, I suggested they form small groups of parents, pupils, and teachers according to their affinity to the topics. Intensive discussions developed within the groups, especially in relation to the spontaneous assignment of parents, pupils, and teachers.

New insights emerged for the first topic, *school subjects*: it was regarded as imperative to do something about the learning atmosphere during French and music lessons. The groups argued about the *structure* and identified a need for action concerning teamwork, the possibility of pupils' integration, the development of individual learning strategies, and the desire for studying without pressure. The third area of subject, *study location*, dealt especially with the classroom design and discomfort, as well as with ideas of changing the classroom environment. The topic of *autonomy* handled the subjects of motivation by goal-setting and the development of consonance by learning how to take over responsibility. There was also a wish for more approval by the teachers and stronger involvement of the pupils in the lesson-planning process. The fifth team worked on new and enhanced ways of *exchange* between pupils, parents, and teachers. They also discussed learning techniques and regular feedback from teachers to pupils about pupil performance.

After collecting the results the teachers were impressed, as they had assumed before the meeting that the focus would be on the personal conflict between the pupils. They had judged their position as more difficult, as their focus had been primarily on the good conveyance of subject matter. The collected results were very motivating for them, as they could imagine working on these topics with both pupils and parents over the next few weeks. They promised to put the results on display in the staff room in order to report on the successful experience.

The parents were also satisfied at the end of the meeting. Besides dissolving the conflict, they were able to gain an insight into the working atmosphere of the class and the perspectives of the children, and they had the opportunity to work on problem-solving together with the other parties involved. The pupils seemed less surprised but deeply satisfied about their ideas and the possibility to express their thoughts and feelings "at last". The developed topics and the willingness of the teachers to continue to work on these ideas and desires together with the parents gave them the much-needed security that conflicts within class would now be history and that they would achieve their goals.

From the systemic point of view, one could say that the conflict between the pupils had accomplished its task by making it necessary to call for help from outside in order to find solutions in a new setting. From the mediation perspective, it is an example of the fact that the conflict subject at the beginning of the mediation process usually loses its position of primary importance. It became essential within the conflict-clarification process to develop ways to articulate the underlying topics and the associated interests and needs. The arrangement of three groups at the beginning of the meeting, the possibility for everyone involved to speak their mind, the collection of the topics, and the group-spanning work on shared solutions considered the conflict analysis on personal, interpersonal, and systemic levels.

Conclusion

Embedding mediation in a school culture is an objective we should strive to achieve. This attempt is not to be mistaken with making students into conflict helpers. Mediation in school aims at changing the daily culture of the school as an organization towards a new discussion about topics such as conflicts, violence, normative convictions, and communication. The institution/school would get a new "face"—it would be transformed from a knowledge factory into a place of education and culture in an appreciative framework. Schools would thus live up to the expectations of actively taking part in creating the community. This transformation cannot be delegated to the lower levels within schools but has to be regarded as a challenge by the head and by as many participants as possible within the school—that is, teachers and others. School projects in which people have been trained in this way and in which the structure of the school has been changed so that new, sustainable forms of interpersonal contacts have been established give reasons to be optimistic. Together with the personal engagement of teachers and the governing body of the school, and through the use of systemic concepts and mediation, the autonomy of all parties involved would rise simultaneously with appreciation and respectful curiosity for others.

Note

1. In Germany, it is uncommon for pupils to participate in parents' evenings.

CHAPTER FIVE

Giving feelings a voice: the case for emotionally literate schools, with particular reference to a London comprehensive

Elizabeth Scott

> Emotional Literacy (EL) can be defined as the ability to recognise, understand, appropriately express and effectively handle emotional states in ourselves and others.
>
> Peter Sharp (2001)

T he notion that it is somehow bad taste to, metaphorically speaking, "wear your emotions on your sleeve" could be considered to be the essence of Britishness. That "stiff-upper-lip" tradition may well be responsible for inhibiting generations of British children, particularly boys, from exhibiting emotional extremes, notably crying and kissing (certainly) males and (often) females. Furthermore, it may be a major contributor to the lack of communication, spoken and tactile, between couples, families, friends, and enemies for decades.

Some readers may be familiar with Mike Leigh's 2004 film *Vera Drake*, which is about backstreet abortions in London in the 1950s. In the film, when Vera's family realize that carrying out these abortions has been almost a mission for their mother/wife, they are all unable to speak. The four of them—all adults—sit around their kitchen table in utter silence. Their shock and, I would argue, their long training in terms of emotional reactions and responses have left them mute—unable to release all the tension, horror, and confusion within. At the end of the film, we are left to wonder what behaviours will follow, once the tension is allowed to build up. Will it explode like a volcano, or will it gradually rot the inner casing until the face and body wither away in disappointment, shame, and despair?

That inability "to come into tender touch", as D. H. Lawrence put it in *Lady Chatterley's Lover* (1928, ch. 18, p. 296) (which itself, incidentally, was once banned in its original text, until in 1961 the twelve men and women at the obscenity trial found the book worthy to be published), has drilled into generations of British people that somehow they lose dignity, self-esteem, and, above all, strength of character if they allow their emotional casing to crack and readily communicate what they really feel.

In spite of what Shakespeare wrote almost five centuries ago, when at the end of *King Lear* Edgar sums up the moral of the tragedy with the lines: "Speak what we feel, not what we ought to say" (V.iii: 323), we have still continued to be conned by the myth that to contain emotion somehow benefits both giver and receiver by building up a kind of intensity within. There is the general acceptance that the understatement is more empowering in the decision not to disclose the true nature of what is held within, by allowing the individual the flexibility to modify before finally stating and by somehow strengthening the emotion because it is not disclosed—as if, by saving within, you somehow accrue interest on your emotional capital.

Some may find this attractive, but I would like to explore a different and, I believe, infinitely more satisfying and fulfilling way forward. Although many take refuge in the more traditional choice of pathway, which allows the individual to "sit on an emotional fence"—another cultural characteristic!—we would like to share with you the development of the Emotional Literacy (EL) project that I was involved with in London.

The comprehensive school in question is situated in an affluent area of London, where many, but by no means all, residents opt for private education for their children. The school's 1,400-strong student population, though, is a living example of the cross-section of society in which a myriad of ethnic and economic groups is represented. The school has spawned famous authors, politicians, and artists, but for us its greatness lies in the fact that, before we ever started working there, it was an emotionally literate school. In a word, it could be described as "organic" and a truly inclusive school. By this I mean that the school embraced and included those students who, for any number of reasons, might have been educated in smaller units, each exclusively designed and tailored for a certain special need. An inclusive school would, typically, see all students with individual special needs, and therefore its curriculum and ethos would be designed to include all.

At the school in question, there is a general acceptance, on the part of all staff, that the only real discipline that endures and changes children into responsible adults is self-discipline. This, combined with a culture of a positive approach to behaviour management and a "can-do" attitude on the part of all staff, provided a solid foundation on which to develop EL within the school.

The project began in the late summer of 2001, when the school chose to use two of its INSET days to look at different models for its pastoral programme. The challenge was how to achieve consistency, a phenomenon that plagues all educational institutions. This, of course, is a nigh impossible task, for to imagine that clear messages can be delivered identically by copious different individuals, each with his or her unique body language and character, age, and current stress level, to name but a few variables, is indeed a bridge too far. The need to strive for consistency, though, is soundly grounded in the philosophy that clear messages make for increased feelings of security within students, which in turn lead to better performance and a more rounded development of each individual. Maybe the most that can be achieved is a willingness among staff to be consistent and a maintenance of procedures. However, it is a tribute to the management of this school that they understood and accepted that they would be able to maximize the effect of this if they encouraged the staff to develop their EL and provided training and time for them to facilitate this.

Consequently, during this INSET weekend, they included presentations to introduce EL and subsequently provided a base for the school to offer an accredited EL Certificate for staff who wanted to explore and understand and develop the issues in both academic and practical contexts, as well as further INSET days for all staff. The take-up for the Certificate included those from senior management, teachers, and support staff.

The programme offered an opportunity to learn key skills and frameworks for applying EL in school against a background and ethos of inclusion for all students, no matter how challenging their behaviour issues. The growing pressure to find solutions to these personal and social difficulties, which can interfere so much with a child's capacity to learn, generated the commitment to the programme. The development of the programme coincided with research into human EL, pioneered by Daniel Goleman (1995), and the recognition that it is highly significant in achieving greater success, as well as being the foundation for personal satisfaction especially in the development of self-esteem and self-confidence.

The learning approach of the programme included the following aspects:

▹ theoretical—with the participant learning the underpinning theories and frames of reference
▹ experiential, where participants learn from one another as they practise skills in the modules, tutorials, and learning sets
▹ action-based research in the participants' workplace/home relevant to EL and self-esteem assessment and development
▹ feedback using emotional intelligence measures before and after the programme
▹ modelling of all EL building skills, principles, values, and attitudes by tutors during the learning process
▹ a reading list, which supports both the theoretical and the practical aspects of the programme
▹ case studies, which add value to the understanding of an application
▹ a Learning Log for reflection and consolidation of learning.

The programme process was run over eleven contact days throughout the course of an academic year, using the medium of workshops. The responses included an "own situation analysis" at the beginning and again at the end of the programme; a report on the applied action learning project; a Learning Log and an Action

Learning Skills Analysis, and evaluation of all EL skills and attitudes learnt and practised during the programme.

To look more closely at two of the above, the Learning Log was an ongoing, regularly maintained record of work undertaken personally and professionally during the programme, which in turn reflected how the students' developing knowledge and implementation of EL theories, attitudes, and skills was impacting, or not, on their activities. To take one example:

The traffic warden sequence

This occurred at the time of the Soccer World Cup in the summer of 2002. I had been delivering a workshop all day in Bristol and was now a passenger in a car travelling back to London.

It was the rush hour and there was heavy traffic, so we were caught in a jam and were moving very slowly. In this situation, though, it was beneficial, because it gave us the opportunity to view the whole incident and experience more than we might otherwise have done.

It was the day of the England–Argentina match, and three hours previously England had—somewhat unexpectedly—been triumphant. Many were out on the streets celebrating. We were just about to pass a vehicle, which was parked illegally on a red line. Two traffic wardens were busily engaged in noting down all its particulars before awarding the dreaded parking ticket. On the opposite side of the street, three football supporters, very happy and waving an English flag, suddenly spotted what the wardens were doing. With smiles on their faces, not being aggressive in the slightest and in the best of humours, they called out to them:

"You can't do that! England WON!"

Until then, I had never seen traffic wardens smile, or even display a positive human emotion, but the expressions of these two suddenly broadened out into enormous grins and began to chuckle. The three supporters danced—literally—across the street and approached them, still in good humour. One of them took the pens/pencils of the wardens and threw them into the bushes. (I later saw one of them retrieve them for the wardens.)

By this time, the wardens, themselves were laughing, their mission in ruins, but they looked very happy. They just gave up and were glad to do so. Their point seemed pointless; the supporters had proved theirs . . . and nobody was hurt!

Whether or not they tried again, I don't know, although I hope not, but to see a positive human emotion on the faces of the traffic wardens and to witness the way that the supporters pitched their protest so appropriately was a joy. All of us in the car were laughing too, and when I later recounted the incident to my son in Greece on the telephone, he too laughed out loud.

This was a triumph for joy over bureaucracy. Lovely! Plus I, not a fan of football, let alone its supporters, experienced total admiration for the way these three handled the situation. It was perfect and I have to admit it—quite humbling, but it gave me great joy.

Turning to the outcome or what I learned from this experience—apart from not belittling the necessary celebrations of football supporters—I learnt consciously to recognize that sometimes the knock-on effect of these celebrations can have the most unexpected and positive results as well as give others the chance to smile and enjoy. I also learnt that the way the supporters handled the wardens—not critically, but with joy—was infectious and entirely appropriate.

Moving on to subsequent actions and plans to do something better, which was the third requirement of the Learning Log, I could summarize this in endeavouring to be more careful in my judgements of others—not all football supporters are hooligans!—and also to be more careful to approach a situation in which I may feel threatened, in a solution-focused way that would permit all participants to enjoy finding common ground and giving all a chance of a better day.

To expand on a second of the modules for the EL Certificate, I want to look more closely at the applied action project. This was action-based research carried out at the participant's workplace or home and was essentially focused on EL and self-esteem assessment and development. I chose to complete this section of the course at the school in question and carried out some group work with four students aged 12–13 years. These students had been identified and referred by their teachers as needing extra help with their social interactions both with their peers and adults in the school, because their social skills, as demonstrated in the classroom, were frequently so inappropriate that they inhibited learning. In addition, the students were the subject of teacher criticism, due to the inappropriate nature of their social skills, and this criticism tended to create problems, manifested in unacceptable behaviour. Consequently, the students experienced various degrees of feelings of isolation and exclusion. Therefore, it almost goes without saying that the focus for the group was "Emotionally Literate Social Skills".

Within the group, though, the individual differences varied considerably. For example, one spectrum of difference ranged from the exhibition of comparatively immature (in terms of child development) behaviour to sophisticated and articulate reasoning that searched for more time and space to satisfy the need to express thoughts and responses.

I began this chapter with the premise that the development of social skills is inextricably bound up with EL because the exchanges between people, no matter what the context, involve an exchange of emotions as well as practical information. The more successfully I can translate (and convey) the emotional part of the message, the easier communication between people becomes. Here I return to the central theme of improved communication between human beings. An example we encounter as teachers every day is in posing a question to any class we teach regarding the information we have been exploring with them during a lesson. What we want when we ask a question in class is a student who answers with body language and tone of voice that convey to us: "I want to get the right answer", "This is a very interesting question and I'm going to do my best to answer it with grace and enthusiasm", "I respect you and I want to answer your question respectfully".

Following on from this, it would be expected that a student would express pleasure at attaining the correct answer, and the teacher too would have the opportunity to mirror this emotion. In order for this two-way communication to take place effectively, we have to approach the students with the same respect, attention, and intention—otherwise it seems unfair to expect the process to go on only one way. Both the teacher and the student have to listen to one another in order to convey their willingness and readiness to engage in the learning process together. Being able to use active listening skills effectively is an essential ingredient for success in any class. It is both therapeutic and a facilitative.

Katherine Weare (2000, p. 5) put it like this: " One of the most powerful ways we can demonstrate our empathy, genuineness and respect is through actively listening to others. Being listened to in an active way is a wonderful experience."

All students in the group were observed in class before the sessions began, and these observations were repeated after the programme was completed. Then, once the sessions were under way, we preceded each aspect of the social skills programme with a "Feelings Check", enabling the students to check their feelings prior to the interaction. They were also invited to do this same exercise at the close of the interaction. This exercise is fundamental to development in EL, and by the time the students reached this section of the sessions, they were familiar with tuning in to their feelings. At the same time, this exercise was validating the importance of listening to your feelings regularly and objectively, which was an additional skill I wanted them to get into the habit of doing. It helped participants start to focus on their current activity and let go of things that had happened to them en route to the meeting. It also helped everyone in the group, including myself, to have a bit of background to what kind of mood everyone else was in, thus giving a context to any exchanges they might have with one another. This activity set up a situation for feelings to be recognized, understood, verbalized, and shared. It also enabled good listening skills to be practised and conveyed respect, honesty, and empathy. These three qualities then each became the subject of a subsequent session.

We also chose to establish the habit of an activity called "Wow, How, Now". This would always take place just before the end of every session and acted like another mini check-out. It involved each participant—again, including myself—reviewing the things that had been talked about, learnt, and experienced and identifying:

> which thing had made the biggest impression—the *Wow*
> which thing had taught them a *How*
> which thing out of all the things they may have learnt would they put into practice *Now*.

The responses by the group could have been the same, or sometimes all were different—it didn't matter. There were no right or wrong answers, and everyone's views were respected. The point of the exercise was to allow time for reflection and consolidation.

The subject matter of the sessions, besides honesty, empathy, and respect included an early session on feelings, thoughts, and behaviour, which aimed to reinforce new learning that listening to feelings is a good idea before leaping into action. Also, it aimed to give the students knowledge about the links between thoughts, feelings, and behaviours.

The specific social skills sessions, which took place towards the end of the programme, were more directly related to practical situations for which the students needed to practise the appropriate skills. The issues addressed in these sessions included those that had previously caused friction between teacher and student as well as between student and student in the classroom. Having time and space to have coaching and practice in these skills empowered the students in their quest of modifying their behaviour. Their confidence increased as they recognized the skills they already had, but which they had tended to manage inappropriately from time to time. They became aware that the way they felt before they exchanged words with any teacher or students could make a big difference to how they managed thereafter.

One other issue that I want to raise at this point is the importance of the environment for the sessions. Schools are busy places, and the likelihood of acquiring the same quiet place, with a warm, restful atmosphere is sometimes a tall order. At the school in question, however, I was fortunate to be able to hold each session in the Student Support Centre (SSC), a house in the school grounds, which had the atmosphere of being half-way between a school and a home. It was quiet and was viewed by students as a haven of comparative peace, which added to their feelings of security and trust. In addition, for any such group work it is important for the environment where it is carried out to be:

> the same place every time
> relatively private and where interruptions are blocked
> as comfortable as possible, or customized in some way that marks it out as "ours". It must not be an uncared for area of the school or an open area where activities can be overheard or seen.

Evaluating the programme

It is important to recognize the difficulties involved in evaluating the programme. For example, what a student might see or feel as a positive change—such as having a better understanding of themselves—might not be seen as such by a teacher. A teacher may be pleased with the student making more attempts to answer questions, whereas a student may not see that as a priority her or she was aiming for. Then again, parents may have "fewer phone calls from school" as a marker. Nevertheless, it is important to try to get some measure of distance travelled during the time spent on a course such as this.

In this case, though, it was decided on giving similar questionnaires to the students involved, their parents, and their teachers. In this way, we could pick up differences of perception as well as areas in which they all saw differences. Some of the questions I asked were subjective. For instance, "What were your feelings about you/your son/your student joining the social skills group?"

It was interesting, in this case, to read the varying responses from different people. Teachers tended to be either positive or relieved, and the students tended to be nervous. All teachers saw the group as a positive move and thought that social skills were essential for success in life. The students tended to value the opportunity to discuss and explore their feelings in the Feelings Check and be in an atmosphere of more openness and where they felt valued more individually.

Answers to the questionnaire also showed up some important gaps in opportunity. For example, the question: "Did you have the opportunity to discuss any of the issues outside the group?" showed that there were very few opportunities to do just this. Some students discussed them with their mothers, but most teachers did not have or make a chance to do this. In contrast, there were comments from other adults that the students seemed keen and willing to talk about their feelings when situations occurred in school. They were obviously open to using this strategy having learnt it—what was missing was the opportunity and understanding from other adults.

The acid test of the programme lies in its effectiveness over time. Skills such as those discussed need to be reinforced and encouraged consistently to really become new social habits. For this reason, the students who come from a school such as this comprehensive, where there is a whole-school approach to EL, fare better. They are in a situation where the staff they deal with all have an understanding and appreciation of what is being achieved and know that being aware of feelings is a core part of this. For others, the knowledge they gain will be lost unless it is reinforced, and for yet another group, the knowledge will lie somewhere in their memory banks only to emerge when they are older and have a different perspective. Sometimes, it seems like an act of faith to run these groups, although it is comforting that the students always seem to want "more".

On a wider perspective, in other school environments the challenge is of how to persuade teachers entrenched in traditional approaches that EL isn't "just another fashion that will go away". Comparative studies between educational systems in other countries serve to demonstrate just how powerful the school can be in passing on an endemic culture. Just to take an example from my experience, an understanding of why in social settings British people tend to line up more than do people in many other cultures is because this was reinforced with them constantly at school! So, in my view, if schools are more emotionally literate, then the students as adults may value the importance of listening to their feelings in communication with others.

The new UK legislation and initiatives by the government regarding EL in Britain are now mandatory in primary schools and are currently being rolled out into secondary schools. Emotional Literacy is designed to underpin the whole curriculum, rather than being seen as another thing that teachers have to "do". Teachers are more likely to be persuaded by training in psychological and emotional functioning and prospective teachers may already have EL as a premise if they have an input in their training in child development, which includes the development of the brain. If the expectation that schools, students, and their teachers are more healthy if they are emotionally literate is there as a given, this would have far-reaching consequences when it comes to communication between individuals.

Hopefully, it will lead to more satisfying and fulfilling relationships between individuals and families, and students and their teachers. Relationships that are based on the certain knowledge that words and actions are precipitated by feelings and that providing real time, space, and consideration to give these feelings a voice can, in fact, lead to a deeper understanding of why people feel angry/sad/joyous/frightened/elated/violent/quiet/fulfilled— and so the list of feelings goes on. It can avoid misunderstandings, resentments, and so many inappropriate and unnecessary actions that only compound the problems and decrease communication between individuals. If feelings are "checked" and time is taken to understand them, the pathway to learning can become unblocked, in the same way that a struggling pilgrim might feel when trying to hack his or her way through a forest of thorns and suddenly, as with the Prince in the children's story of *Sleeping Beauty* (written by Charles Perrault in 1697), the thorns part and the way ahead is clear daylight. When there is clear communication between individuals, the foundation is there for trust to develop—trust on which young, eager minds can become illuminated through knowledge about the world they live in with a positive frame of mind and ready to contribute to their communities. They can learn to use the skills that they have learnt at school to make our world a better place, and in so doing they might experience a sense of self-fulfilment.

Jumping off that fence and being not only unafraid, but also confident to use what we feel to be a tool for positive communication, is an approach that involves resilience and risk. I hope I have demonstrated that it is eminently worth it.

CHAPTER SIX

Working and learning together: a collaboration between the Tavistock Clinic and New Rush Hall School

Gillian Ingall & Maureen Smyth

T he aim of this chapter is to describe the collaboration between our two institutions, the New Rush Hall School and the Tavistock and Portman NHS Foundation Trust (T&P). This collaboration provides a helpful model for developing other CAMHS and educational collaborations, in light of the UK government's recent imperative for the delivery of children's services to be undertaken in an integrated and joined-up way, with equality of access being one of the overriding principles (*Every Child Matters*, 2004).

We first describe the history of the collaboration and the development of a bespoke professional development course delivered at New Rush Hall School by visiting lecturers from the T&P. We consider the impact on both learners and teachers—including the costs and benefits to both institutions and what might be learned to support other developing partnerships. Finally, we consider the lessons of our collaboration and how these might be generalized to other situations.

Context

In the year 2000, schools in England were struggling to implement around three hundred and sixteen new government initiatives. New Rush Hall School, an outer London all-age mixed day special school for children with behavioural, emotional, and social difficulties (BESD), found that all its training time was allocated to implementing the Literacy Strategy, Numeracy Strategy, and Information and Communication Technology Strategy, leaving little time to understand the E in BESD. The collaboration between the two institutions dates from that time, when the school's managers were looking for a way to ensure that the emotional needs of pupils and the training needs of staff could be addressed in a way that did not deflect from the more conventional aspects of the curriculum.

At the same time, the school was recovering from an Ofsted (Office of Standards in Education) inspection (February 1998) which, although it produced a positive report, left staff feeling bruised and misunderstood. With hindsight, the school's wish to understand this experience and recover from it may have added to the motivation to look for external support and further understanding of the emotional impact of the inspection on the school community.

In 2001, the Tavistock Clinic had a national training contract through the Department of Health to deliver training to a range of health and other professionals in the area of child & adolescent mental health. At that time, there were a number of centres in different parts of the country already delivering university-validated, Tavistock, postgraduate-level courses. There was a desire to develop the training portfolio to include courses more easily accessible to the workforce who might not have the prerequisite qualifications for a postgraduate course. Within the child psychotherapy discipline, this meant finding ways of bringing psychoanalytic thinking to a wider range of Tier 1 and Tier 2 professionals and work settings. This coincided with a wish within the discipline to develop a range of access and introductory courses to psychoanalytic thinking—an escalator of training—with one aim being to broaden the traditional composition of the child psychotherapy profession.

The University of East London/Tavistock Clinic postgraduate Certificate/Diploma/Masters course in Emotional Factors in Learning and Teaching: Counselling Aspects in Education had been delivered and developed for over 30 years, but only at the Tavistock Clinic. The course, based on a psychoanalytic framework for thinking, was held within the child psychotherapy discipline, with professionals from other disciplines contributing to the teaching and lecturing, including aspects of systemic thinking about education.

The collaboration

In 1999, the course organizers were contacted by a former course graduate, who was then Head of Outreach Services at New Rush Hall, requesting that the first year of the course be delivered at the school. This challenging request provided an ideal opportunity to deliver the course elsewhere.

While it was impossible to do this with a full programme of visiting lecturers, due to the distance from the T&P and the proposed after-school timings, it was agreed that a version of the first year of the course would be created for New Rush Hall. It was to be taught in the school, which was at the centre of the BESD service, and offered initially to all teachers and learning support assistants (LSAs), as well as the senior managers working within the school and outreach service. The new, adapted course consisted of 30 seminars over the academic year, each involving a reading and a case presentation. The weekly readings introduced a psychoanalytic framework for thinking about the emotional tasks of learning at different stages of development. There were to be occasional whole-course discussions, often based around a video, and an ambitious programme of three Saturday INSET days.

A final planning meeting was scheduled at the school on 11 September 2001. By the time the meeting had started, dramatic and unbelievable events were unfolding in Manhattan, as two aeroplanes were flown into the Twin Towers. As the meeting processed the news, in everyone's mind was the question of the impact such terrible destructiveness by the adult world would have on the vulnerable and often self-destructive pupils in the school.

New Rush Hall School is housed in part of a large, ex-secondary school with a playing field and grounds in front, of a size not often seen in Inner London. The atmosphere is of a well-cared-for primary school, with large airy classrooms, square windows, high ceilings, and work pinned up on the walls. There was evidence in the facilities for the pupils and staff of the capacity of the school to harness resources for the benefit of the school. The financial prowess proved invaluable in supporting the ongoing development of the collaboration.

Once the course began, the light and airy school building soon became filled, during the work discussion presentations, with accounts of painful and difficult encounters with troubled and troubling young people. A further rather incongruous feature of teaching at the school continues to be the loud often harmonious noises coming from the Redbridge Music Service based above on the first floor of the building and catering for an altogether more materially and socially privileged section of the school-aged population in the area.

In the first year, 75% of the school staff attended the course, and they were allocated to three seminar groups, each lead by a child & adolescent psychotherapist from the Tavistock Clinic. Each group comprised a range of staff including LSAs, school and outreach teachers, and senior managers, a complex composition likely to create anxiety for all concerned. Could a probationary teacher and a head teacher work alongside each other to present difficult classroom encounters without feeling too exposed? Would the group be safe enough to manage a situation in which individuals' differing capacity to engage with new learning would cut across their role or status within the school? How would the range of difference in prior formal educational experience be accommodated when texts with varying degrees of difficulty were required reading? Would staff be able to use their first-hand experience of being students on the course to understand further the emotional challenges of learning faced by their pupils? Staff's capacity to manage the exposure of the work discussion setting over time, supported by the seminar leader, may have offered a way of further processing the experience of over-exposure during inspection.

The reading programme contained a variety of texts ranging from the accessible writings of Isca Salzberger-Wittenberg (1970; Salzberger-Wittenberg, Henry, & Osborne, 1983) and Sue Kegerreis (1995), to more dense and less applied papers, which needed more than one seminar devoted to them. Course members showed impressive commitment to tackle these unfamiliar texts. Two texts in particular stand out for the interest they generated. Esther Bick's paper "The Experience of the Skin in Early Object-Relations" (1968), to which reference was frequently made, fascinated course members, and they struggled with it, frequently returning to it throughout the course. In the 1996 issue of the *Journal of Child Psychotherapy* devoted to the work of Winnicott, Mikardo's commentary in her paper "Hate in the Countertransference" provided a powerful relief to seminar members. Mikardo writes about her early days as a "fresh-faced graduate", working at the Cotswold Community:

> One thing I had not been at all prepared for when I arrived was the altruistic, loving impulses which had propelled me towards the Community—some aspects of which I would now recognize as "rescue fantasies"—could be overturned at times by feelings of extreme anger with my charges, verging on murderousness. [Mikardo, 1996, p. 399]

This particular commentary linked directly to the everyday emotional experiences of staff and, in time, allowed discussion of the turbulent and mixed emotions that arose in staff when, for example, restraint was used on a pupil.

Developing an appropriate reading programme has pointed to the need for more applied psychoanalytic writings on the teaching and learning process. Biddy Youell's book *The Learning Process* (2006), written as a result of her long involvement in both the original course in the Tavistock and the development of the course in New Rush Hall School, as well as work with many other groups of teachers, has been a very welcomed new contribution to this field. Child psychotherapists teaching on the course continue to face the challenging task of applying an understanding of psychoanalytic theory in a way that makes it accessible to course members—for example, how to make helpful links between an understanding of oedipal constellations written about in the papers and issues of inclusion and exclusion present for the pupils, parents, teachers, and learning assistants as described in work discussion presentations and evidenced in experiential exercises.

The work discussion component of the course proved extremely challenging to some course members and at times challenging to everyone. This has also been the experience of the work discussion component of the Tavistock-based course. At New Rush Hall, resistance to tackling the work sometimes took the form of an attempt to use the seminar as a debriefing session, which was already catered for in the school. The prompt starting time of the seminars was often compromised by the day's events, and it took time to establish the helpfulness of maintaining the boundaries of the seminars. Members would arrive, often at the end of stressful and exhausting days, wanting a break and not always initially ready to tackle a difficult piece of reading or listen to a presentation. Some members struggled to be able to present in the mixed groups containing management, school-based teachers, outreach teachers, and LSAs. Some struggled with keeping the boundary, wanting to discuss their personal rather than their professional dilemmas. Over time, course members became more confident in the insight and support they would gain from the group when they presented.

The following extract from a work discussion presentation involving a secondary pupil gives a flavour of the challenging situations staff grappled with in their work. The missing expletives perhaps demonstrate the initial uncertainty of course members about how much the seminar leaders could bear.

Tony walked in that morning and said, "I am not going into assembly. It is **** and you can't force me. My uncle said you couldn't touch me, otherwise he will come and sort you out", he added. I told him he had to make a sensible choice and that he very well knew the consequences if he did not attend. Tony initially stayed out of the assembly but joined after five minutes.

The presentation went on to describe how Tony found it difficult to settle when lessons began. An offer of help was made by the teacher and quickly rejected by Tony. The LSA took over the task of trying to convince him to settle down. This seemed to further infuriate Tony, who began throwing pencils, then books, on to the floor. He was asked to stop, otherwise he would need to work outside, as his behaviour was unsafe and put other pupils at risk.

Every pupil was seated except pupil Tony. It was the first lesson of the day. I asked him to sit down like all the other pupils, and the response was, "You don't tell me what to do, you *******. I do what I want". "Why are you so rude to me?" I asked him.

Tony started to move round the class, tapping the tables. "Sit down you *****", shouted one pupil. "**** you", Tony responded. "You may not use that kind of language", I reminded Tony. "If you need time out then ask for it, but do not disrupt the class." "I am not doing any work today. I do what I want", Tony added. I reminded him that choices were being made here, and there would be consequences.

"I don't care", he emphasized, "and you can't stop me or else I will punch you in the face." I decided that it was time for Tony to be led out of the room to work in isolation. He resisted, but we managed to take him out of the room. He shouted and struggled as we held him using the single-elbow technique, leading him out of the room. "Leave me alone, you ******* *****, and you ******* ****." He screamed and kicked objects around him. He was finally led out of the room. "What is wrong this morning?" I asked him. "Why have you decided to behave this way?", I added. "Leave me alone", he shouted, kicking the wall and the door. "I hate this ******* school." I then asked him if he had any problem I could help him with, or maybe he could discuss it with the LSA. I then returned to the rest of the pupils and continued with the lesson.

The presentation described an increasingly angry and distressed Tony. At the end of the lesson, Tony calmed and helped clear up the mess and made up the work. He then sat down and looked sad.

"OK, how can we help you, Tony?", I asked. "Do you know I will soon be leaving home?", said Tony. "Where are you

going?", we asked. "I don't know", he replied. "I fought with
my Mum on Sunday and hurt her hand. She can't do anything.
What happens if they take you to a foster home?" "To be hon-
est, I don't know," I replied, "but I could find out for you." "My
Mum can't force me out of the house", he said.

We then went on to discuss what had really happened at home and
Tony's worries about what might happen next.

Material like this allowed further insight into both the emotional
state of the child and the impact the child had on the members of
staff. It also allowed a more general discussion on the impact on
staff of restraining children, as well as the likely impact on the
children, suggesting they could exercise choice in a situation that
is already felt to be out of control by both the staff member and the
child. The honesty in the presentation gave permission for other
members to acknowledge the difficult and uncomfortable feelings
that arose for them in confrontations with pupils. To insist a child
in this emotionally charged state had a choice, when both child and
adult already anticipated a physical restraint, was both provocative and despairing and seemed to confirm that no adult help was
on hand. Interestingly, after about three years of the course being
delivered in the school, the then Head of the Secondary Department commented on the significant decrease in restraints being
used in his section of the school, which he understood as a result
of the impact of the course.

The third component of the New Rush Hall School course was
the INSET days, which took place on three Saturdays. The idea
was to allow for an opportunity for lecturers to visit the course and
to use their input to consolidate the learning that was beginning
to take place. The fact that the INSET days were to take place on
Saturdays also meant that the course tutors needed to find a way
to include a playful element in the teaching and learning on these
days, enough to compete with the usual Saturday morning tasks.
In fact, they have also proved to be very enjoyable and stimulating
to design for course tutors.

The following format to the INSET Days developed: breakfast,
then a lecture, followed by a seminar with a small-group task that
linked the content of the lecture to the psychoanalytic content of

the lecture to the day-to-day work experience of the participants. A lecture on endings, for example, was followed by an exercise considering how endings are managed in the participants' workplaces and how they might review and improve this, following the insight gained from the lecture. One group of teachers from the school decided that rather than sending pupils a postcard from their holidays, they would make a book for pupils to have with them over the long summer break to remind them of what they had achieved in the previous term and of when the school would start again.

The school always provided a welcoming lunch, adding to the pleasure of the INSET days. The afternoons were devoted to experiential learning. One memorable example followed a lecture and exercises based on group dynamics. For the afternoon session, participants were divided into three groups. The first consisted of all the senior managers; the second, a randomly selected small group of three; and the third, the remaining twelve. The task was to redesign the staffroom of the school in order to improve it. All groups were provided with the same materials and access to the same external support, in order to complete their task. Halfway through the task, each group was asked to choose an observer who would observe one of the other groups. Fascinating differences emerged between the capacity of the different groups to engage in this creative task, based on group size and composition. The observers also found their task fascinating, noticing the internal dynamics of the groups, which they sensitively fed back to the interest of all.

In recent years, the course has included just two Saturday INSET days, as course members found the commitment to three Saturdays difficult. Instead, one of the weekly seminar groups takes place at the Tavistock Centre, where participants are sometimes joined by members of other related courses. This, too, has proved a difficult but interesting experience. The experience of being members of different course groups inside and outside the institution is used as a basis for exploration, highlighting issues of inclusion and exclusion.

We have started to see these experiential events on the INSET days as a form of applied group relations learning, with a great need for an opportunity for playfulness, kindly leadership, and ample time to reflect on how to apply the learning to a school setting. Each INSET day ends with a plenary session to consolidate the learning. Course tutors continue to struggle to get the balance right.

Although all school staff were invited to attend the Saturday training events, few did. Looking back at this, we can think of it as another indication of how powerful the dynamic of inclusion/exclusion is and the impact it has had on the formation of the course. Not only has it often been the theme for one of the INSET days, but it has also emerged in other ways.

The outreach team in many ways acutely experience this dynamic in their everyday work. Not all members of the team joined the first year of the course, leaving team members in different positions with regard to the learning on the course. We were fascinated to learn that they instigated a preliminary reading group in their team meetings, so that all members had studied the texts and discussed them together, with no one being left out.

Lessons in learning and teaching

The experience of being the learner, while often exhilarating, also inevitably proved an anxious and painful experience for all course members. In various ways, individual members of the course employed a series of defences against being in the learner role when this felt too exposing, including being absent on the day of their presentation or presenting material at one remove from actual interactions with pupils. In addition, rather like the first child born to a family, members of the first cohort of the course had to suffer from the inexperience of the course tutors, who were yet to know how helpful a learning experience the course would be.

The new learning that the course brought to the school did not come without costs. There was thinking to be done, but there was no magic. It was slow and painful and, as in all schools, was understood by some more than others. The children were still difficult to manage and the staff still challenged. Talking and thinking about new ways of working raised expectations for some staff that there would be a greater awareness about what was happening in interactions between staff and children. It was provocative to some staff that the gap between a theoretical understanding and the everyday reality of working with children at times felt so wide, and they left the course, angry and disappointed.

The school was also engaged in discussions about their primary purpose. Was their role to enable mainstream schools to function better, or were special schools just a mini-version of mainstream education with the same constraints and high academic expectations—"mainstream school with toast"? Or could a truly alternative educational experience be offered to some very troubled children and thereby enhance their life chances? The collaboration between the T&P and the school was based on learning, but how would it be known who had learned what and what kind of learning was valued? This resonated with the school's previous experience of inspection and the lack of value placed on understanding compared to data and statistics.

Over time, a working partnership was established. The visiting lecturers brought a learning opportunity and new understanding; the school provided a venue, hospitality, organized the financing and the local administration of the course, and also provided some core textbooks. This working relationship was also "fed" by regular meetings between the organizers of the partnership, affording an opportunity to get to know each other. This fostered a great respect for each side of the partnership as an understanding developed of the preoccupations of the others' professional lives.

The collaboration started with two different professions coming together and negotiating a relationship to their mutual benefit. For a long time, the school felt that it was a willing and fortunate recipient of expert knowledge and expertise and that the benefits were one-way. Initially, the long, rather unpredictable journey to the school from the T&P, together with the course being run when many child psychotherapists had patients, meant that staffing the course proved difficult. There has been a tendency for potential staff to feel that the desirable place to teach is within their training institution, the T&P, and that an outreach version of the main course was a less attractive option. Again, evidence can be seen of the powerful dynamic of inclusion and exclusion. Indeed, the parent course, which has a tradition of coupling experienced teachers with new teachers in the first-year seminars, is thought of as a place to begin teaching, once qualified as a child psychotherapist.

However, those child psychotherapists who started their teaching at New Rush Hall School have found it to be a containing experience, well supported by their more experienced colleagues. The teaching base within the school has felt a grounded way of beginning to tackle the fascinating task of introducing a psychoanalytic framework for thinking to a range of staff working within the New Rush Hall Group and also within other local schools, as the membership of the course has expanded.

For the course organizers, some of the applied reading material chosen for the course has now been included in the reading list of the parent course, as well as some of the more experimental ways of teaching developed for the New Rush Hall INSET days. In fact, the model of course delivery is one that could be exported to other collaborations.

The benefits for the T&P staff have also included clinical ones. One child psychotherapist teaching on the course commented on his increased understanding and confidence in going to school-based reviews for children in therapy. He felt he was much more able to have a fruitful dialogue with teachers and to reach a shared understanding of a child.

Generalizing from the collaboration

At the 2005 Paris Conference on Child & Adolescent Mental Health in Educational Settings, the collaboration presented the experience of working together, which interested participants. It was noticeable that not many educationalists were represented, either as delegates or as presenters, and also, and perhaps connected, how there seemed to be evidence of the potential for splitting. Difficulties in the delivery of CAMHS and other similar interventions from an educational base seemed to be easily laid at the door of the educational establishment, rather than within the collaborative relationship or within the inherent difficulties of achieving successful multidisciplinary and multi-modal working within CAMHS teams. Further thought about of the nature of "visitor–host" relationships may well be productive.

So far, the collaboration has been between an educational establishment and a training venture delivered by child psychotherapists and recently extended into a clinical provision. It is possible, therefore, only to attempt to understand the visitor–host relationship from this experience, rather than from the perspective of a partnership involving educationalists and a multidisciplinary team, with the added complications of professional rivalries but also the greater range of skills and provision. However, it is hoped that some of the ways that the collaboration has been nourished and the difficulties addressed will still be applicable to the more complicated relationships described above.

One way of thinking about the dynamics of a visitor–host relationship is to consider how it is revealed within the working relationship between parents and mental health clinicians. It could equally be considered in regard to the relationship between teachers and parents. Mental health clinicians, like teachers, act *in loco parentis* for the time the children are in their care and parents are not present. It is in the interest of the children for there to be an established parental alliance if children are to progress, develop, and feel understood. Getting alongside parents and listening to their concerns and preoccupations about their children, as well as being interested in and discussing similarities and differences in how the child is seen, allows a working towards a jointly held picture of the child. Getting to know something of the culture of the child's family also enables a more confident partnership around the child. However, parents, like CAMHS professionals developing a service based within a school, have to negotiate the different culture of the school from the home as well as their different primary tasks in relation to the child, while sharing responsibility for the child's development. Parents also bring with them their previous experiences of CAMHS or other "helping" services, so this is a complicated situation for both parties to negotiate and one that cannot be either rushed or avoided if sufficient trust is to develop.

Similarly, difficulties in the collaboration, such as establishing the boundaries around the seminar times, could only gradually be negotiated when trust in course tutors was established. Otherwise, the time boundaries of the seminar, and the exposure of the presentation and the discussion, would be seen as unhelpful and persecutory. These difficulties are compounded by being visitors and not working on one's own ground. In addition, there are striking differences between the two institutions' primary tasks. When there was sufficient evidence that insight gained in the seminars supported good learning relationships, then a trusting alliance was established between course members and tutors.

What has been learned about the collaboration is that it takes time to develop and there are no shortcuts. Using the opportunity to prepare for the Paris presentation was in itself an opportunity to develop the collaboration and is something to be recommended. It required effort to make time to reflect together on the joint, shared and different experiences. Equally important was the opportunity to think about and develop a clear understanding of and respect for the primary task and the different cultures of both institutions. This means that when conflicts occur they can be understood, minimizing the risk of splitting between the two organizations.

Postscript

Struggles bear fruit, and as a result of this collaboration the school has gone on to commission a school-based child psychotherapy service from the Tavistock Clinic. The course, now recruiting in its eighth year, is well established within Redbridge and is available to staff from New Rush Hall School and other schools and services within the borough and beyond.

CHAPTER SEVEN

Supporting children diagnosed with a developmental disorder: advantages of family home interventions for school integration

Patrice Govaerts

M any studies have shown the importance of environmental factors in child psychological and social development. The Itinerant Educational Service (SEI: Service Educatif Itinérant) was created in Geneva to respond to the needs of supporting children and families by offering family and systemic interventions. Our psychological interventions for children from 0 to 6 years of age (until school integration) are designed to be provided in our clients' homes. Our team works with children with developmental disorders (e.g., psychological, sensory, motor).

Our service provides support for parents and siblings as well as for professionals working directly with these children. In this chapter, which is based on the result of observations and discussions with parents, we describe how a home-based systemic approach can enable families to support their child and creates a solid therapeutic alliance that will prove useful for families to engage with other professionals.

Description of the SEI

The Itinerant Educational Service of Geneva has existed since 1969 and today is made up of a team of 12 psychologists. It offers psycho-educational and therapeutic interventions at home in any situation involving a child of 0–6 years with developmental difficulties. The problems are various and concern as much sensory problems (e.g., blindness, deafness) as congenital problems (hydrocephalus, genetic problems) or problems affecting the entire development (autism). The service also provides support for families at risk (e.g., violence, parental mental illness, divorce). The child is always at the centre of our interventions. Usually informed of the situation by a professional who has spoken of our service to the parents, we wait for the parents to contact us. This is extremely important for the development of a therapeutic alliance.

In about 50% of cases, we intervene in the first year of the child's life, especially if difficulty is noticed at birth. Thirty per cent of requests are made by parents directed towards us by the paediatric service of the Regional Hospital. We follow up more than 200 children and families per year.

The principle of integration and aspects of socialization of the child are part of our priorities. We regularly collaborate with educational services, as one of our primary goals is to make sure that the child is integrated into mainstream education. We are also often the coordinators of a network of multi-agency meetings and carry out core assessments.

Intervention

Our interventions begin after steps are taken by the parents to contact our service. This makes our presence in their home less intrusive. We have noticed that their voluntary involvement is better than if the follow-up at home was imposed. Our follow-ups are always part of a perspective of partnership between the parents and professionals.

The first four sessions help us to gather information about the history of the child and the family, to understand the context of the child, and to explore how the family perceives the problem. In fact, the sociocultural level of the family plays a part in the mode of approaching the child and his or her difficulties as well as the expectations of the care provided. In the first stage, the parents have the opportunity to express their needs.

During a second stage, we build an intervention project, with the parents setting the objectives as well as the means of reaching them. This second phase takes place over a very variable period of time depending on various factors (e.g., the developmental needs of the child, the family context).

It is important to review the objectives regularly in order to adapt them in accordance with the way in which the child and family develop. We therefore regularly offer the opportunity for the parents to express their wishes as well as their degree of satisfaction.

Our mandate for intervention can stretch from the birth of the child until the child is starting school and is adequately integrated in the education setting (between 4 and 6 years). The relay is then taken up by the pluri-disciplinary team linked to the school. We also sometimes steer families towards other professionals (e.g., therapists, clinical psychologists), depending on the identified needs.

In certain situations, our interventions are short, either because of the age of the child or when parents do not want a long-term involvement of our service.

Types of intervention and the frequency and contents of follow-ups (centred on the child and the family)

As psychologists, we offer various psychological interventions. We are always mindful of the stressful experience of parents who have been told that their child is presenting with a developmental disorder. A recent study on the satisfaction of parents (Favez, Métral, & Govaerts, 2008) has shown an extremely high level of satisfaction with the service we offer. However, parents do not always recognize the help and support they receive from us when we are involved. It seems that satisfaction is always an *après-coup* result of our interventions. Understanding the development of their child was often mentioned as very helpful. Most of our psychologists have trained in systemic approaches, allowing them to work on the genogram or the function of the family unit. Our interventions are designed around the child but also around the family. It happens that we need to offer family therapy when we think that can help to resolve family dysfunctions.

As regards our intervention with young children, after the first sessions of observation and evaluation (of the child and the interaction with the parents and/or siblings), we suggest some psycho-educational activities, taking into account the developmental needs of the child.

It is important that the parents are present during these interventions, as not only are they able to convey their knowledge of their child and his or her needs, but it is also an opportunity for parents to model their interaction with their child.

If required, we can orient the child towards more specialist types of therapeutic interventions (e.g., individual psychotherapy, play therapy, speech therapy, occupational therapy). We regularly review the progress of the child, in partnership with the parents (Favez & Métral, 2002).

Our work with the families consists in a systemic understanding of the way the family functions. We explore how the child's problems are perceived and what meaning they have for the family system. It sometimes happens that the balance of the family unit is articulated around the child's disability. Particular care is also attached to the siblings so that they do not suffer from "doing well".

A child who is different (from the ideal of the child held by the parents before his or her birth) can sometimes provoke violent or aggressive reactions on the part of the parents (the fantasy of the death of the child is often present at an unconscious level). Parents may feel a non-acceptance of the child, a form of rejection of an element for which they were not prepared when it happened. It is therefore important for us to provide containment for what the parents have experienced as normal in order to help them to control their guilt. With time, we later notice better ways of investing in the child. This relationship of confidence with the parents requires a strong alliance with the therapist. In fact, it is hard to imagine how difficult it may be for parents to share their feelings of rejection towards their child.

The difference between the child dreamed of and the real child may have such an impact that it is crucial to intervene quickly with such families.

The case of Jules, a 6-month-old boy with Down syndrome, illustrates this issue. His syndrome was not identified during pregnancy. At his birth only his mother had a terrible doubt: did he have Down syndrome? Some of his features made her think of this syndrome. Those around her—husband, family, medical team—reassured her immediately that he didn't have Down syndrome.

However, two days after his birth, a genetic analysis confirmed her fears. The family fell apart: why them? What had they done? Was this reality or a nightmare? In what context could this child, in good health apart from this, be able to integrate in a family unit that already had a child of 3 years?

The intervention helped the family to accept and integrate Jules as part of the family. This took six months. However, the mother had to be hospitalized for a month for serious depression and has been undergoing psychotherapy as well as treatment by antidepressants. Our service has been intervening in this family since the child was 2 months old. They called on us after advice by a geneticist from the hospital. The work consisted mainly in listening to their narrative and helping them to co-create a new narrative. Many difficulties persist, but the narratives of abandonment and death wishes have disappeared. The parents cannot imagine their life without Jules.

Sometimes our interventions begin when the child is older, either because the parents were not ready or did not feel the needed help, or because the child's difficulties became greater as he or she grew up. This is often the case when the child presents a problem that increases with development. The work with the child and with those who surround him is then different.

As mentioned before, the shock of having a child with a significant disability is considerable. Parents are often in despair. The nature of our intervention is therefore to give them hope, and our interventions are guided by the readiness of parents to understand and accept the child's difficulties.

Children with severe behavioural difficulties are also referred to us. These children generally have difficulties in regulating their behaviour. Our interventions in those cases focus on training to first provide a meaning to the presenting behaviour and then explore the various causes that can maintain it.

This type of work is also preventative. We try to get referrals when professionals or parents are concerned that the child's behaviour could deteriorate over time. Our role is to go beyond the "naughty child" label and understand the emotional and family causes of the behaviour.

Advantages of intervention in the home

A specific aspect of our work is the itinerant aspect of our interventions. In fact, we work at the home of the families who request our help or in the place where the child socializes (e.g., nursery, play, school). This aspect includes undeniable advantages due to the variety of information at our disposal because we are at the heart of their family intimacy—their home.

Whereas at our centre in Geneva the family could be tempted to disguise the reality of their daily lives, it is different when they open their doors to us. We are therefore in the presence of a considerable flux of information that will need to be filtered so as to extract the elements useful to understanding the way in which the family functions.

Our range of actions is extremely wide: we can act upon concrete physical aspects of the home that may present physical dangers for a child with a developmental disability.

The following example is a good illustration of the importance of intervening at all levels.

The family (both parents and their two children, aged 1 and 3 years) live in a large flat, with three bedrooms. The parents and the youngest son sleep in one of the bedrooms, while the other son has his own room. The remaining bedroom is full of a number of fitness machines. For several years the older child has had behavioural difficulties, refuses to go to bed, and is aggressive towards his little brother. After going through the family history with the parents, we realize that this situation is more than just a reaction to the arrival of the youngest child. After the "usual" recommendations on the importance of giving time to the elder child and giving value to his role as big brother, we suggested acting on the internal installation of the flat. Each child will have his own room from now on, and rituals will be set up for each one. The parents at first reacted by saying that they only had two bedrooms.

They had simply forgotten the room full of fitness equipment and had never thought of using it as a room for one of their sons. The third bedroom had almost disappeared from their mind, and when a paediatrician had asked them about their flat they had said that they were living in a two-bedroom flat.

This non-exhaustive example serves to illustrate the gap that can exist between reality as expressed by the parents and that as seen by an observer from outside the system.

A notable difference between fieldwork and interventions at the centre resides precisely in the aspects of the way in which reality is presented. Whereas at the centre the therapist constructs his or her representation of the family history according to the words used by the family members, in the home we are at the heart of the place in which the story is being written. We also know that an intervention in the place where the family lives is often easier to pursue for the parents than to transfer advice received outside.

We find that interventions at home are also well suited to parents with mental health problems or with learning disabilities.

Over the years, the value of home interventions has been confirmed by the feedback we receive from parents and professionals alike.

Preventive aspects: different approaches

Home interventions offer many possibilities in terms of prevention. In addition to more traditional therapeutic interventions, visiting families may lead to some innovative interventions. For example, an over-stimulating environment for a child who has difficulties with selecting and processing relevant information from his or her context puts the child at risk of developing significant difficulties in adapting to the environment and complicates the already complex issues that children with developmental delay face everyday. We pay great attention to this sort of "detail" that is potentially harmful for the best development of the child.

> After one home visit and seeing the arrangement of the flat, we could see that all the signs of the baby's family environment led him to believe that he had to remain a small child: lots of baby toys strewn all over the flat, photos of babies everywhere on the walls, babies' bottles, and so on. After noting these elements to the parents, they were able to recognize their difficulty in seeing their child grow, with all that that implied for the child's desire for autonomy. They could not stand the idea that their child could no longer need them to do everything (unconsciously) so that he would need their help with each act of his daily life. The fact of having been able to give words to their actions enabled them to realize the obstacles that they were creating, in spite of themselves, to the development of their child. Several changes were then carried out and the child was able to overcome part of its retardation.

A family approach also enables the prevention of psychological problems in the child with an impediment. In fact, like any child, the child with an impediment builds his personality on the basis of what his environments reflects. He develops an image of himself according to his competence and his difficulties. It is therefore important for him that his successes (at times difficult to perceive) should be noted and recompensed to give him the strength and courage to start again. In this way, we prevent the installation of a psychopathology in addition to the handicaps that are sometimes already very hard to bear.

Preventive work is also carried out around the family unit (notably the siblings). In fact the siblings of a child with considerable developmental problems often suffer from the fact that attention is very much focused on the "problem" child. The arrival of a child with a handicap strongly perturbs the pre-existing family balance and dynamics. We therefore attach very special attention to making sure that each member of the family has a place where he or she feels at ease, one that is recognized by the other members of the family. In order to do this we try to organize regular meetings with all the members of the family.

The prevention of violence in the family also engages our attention. The important alliance with the family has sometimes led to revelations about family violence. Making it possible to allow angry and exhausted parents to express their emotions first provides a relief and then often the search for alternatives to ill-treatment of the members of the family.

Alliance of work and parental satisfaction

A recent study whose detailed results have been published in the magazine *Child Care in Practice* (Favez, Métral, & Govaerts, 2008) has shown a high level of general satisfaction in parents whose child has been followed by the Itinerant Educational Service of Geneva. This result confirms those of several other studies revealing considerable satisfaction in the domain of parents whose child has been followed up early (Lanners & Mombaerts, 2000). A debate is now engaged in determining in what measure this result effectively reflects the general quality of the care provided by the therapists, or whether it is due to other factors such as the impossibility for the families to compare with other situations because of the lack of alternatives at their disposal (Britner & Phillips, 1995).

The working relationship between the psychologist who is providing the interventions and the family is generally good. This gives a favourable prediction for the evolution of the child and the family due to his or her involvement. On occasions, some families do not have particular expectations or worries and decide not to become involved in the work that we propose. Also, parents may contact us just because it has been offered to them and, because they do not want to feel they are "bad parents", they get in touch with us.

It is during the first sessions that these elements appear. To us, it is thus important to respect their decision and, with the agreement of the parents, accordingly to inform the network of care or the therapist who indicated the measure. It is up to them to pursue this further if required.

Ends of follow-up and transitions

Very often, as initial regular interventionists with the families, we create the first links of a relation between the parents and the young child in difficulties with his or her development. Our work takes place over several years in many situations (we sometimes follow certain children from their birth until 4 years at the rate of one session per week). Then we become an integral part of a system in which we are supposed to regulate the links and interactions. Due to this, the end of the follow-up with a family has to be worked on from the first meetings. We must be immediately clear about the limits (as much in time as in content) of our work. In spite of this, real links are formed between the psychologist intervening in the home and the members of the family, and habits are formed. The frequency and regularity of our work invites the families to count on our presence to metabolize the events they are living through. We must be attentive so as not to create dependency on this frequent and regular assistance.

We finish our interventions when the child goes full time to a school adapted to its needs. We ensure that the transition with the new professionals of reference with the child is as harmonious as possible. A specialized school will propose regular assessments (at best monthly) to the families in order to measure the child's evolution and share questions concerning development. Certain reception structures offer regular family meetings.

One of the preventive aspects of our work will consist precisely of an effort to help the parents to overcome the crises they go through themselves or with the resources at their disposal.

Discussion

As described before and in various studies where a meta-analysis on the efficiency of programmes of intervention in the home (Sweet & Appelbaum, 2004), a tendency towards general satisfaction is evident in the patients taken into care. Though the importance of each factor is not yet clearly determined, the intervention in the home responds to a request for help (conscious or unconscious, expressed or not . . .). Many plans and discussions are at present being considered to measure the efficiency of our interventions, apart from the satisfaction of our patients. Many ethical and methodological factors are obstacles at present to the realization of such studies. It is, in fact, difficult to consider not giving our services to certain families just for the purpose of comparing the efficiency of our interventions with other families.

Many advantages are present in psychological work in the home such as that provided by the SEI. This is as much for the family as for the clinician, who has at his or her disposal a margin of manoeuvrability and much important information to help the family. However, this can be perilous if the psychologist allows him/herself to be swamped and contaminated by a family dysfunction as regards relations (e.g., in the case of a family with a psychotic tendency). We do not arrive in terrain already conquered (though the fact that the parents open their door to us is a measure of our welcome); it is up to us to prepare the ground of our intervention by respecting the request for help. Sometimes this request for help only concerns the child with developmental difficulties. A systemic approach suggests a global vision of a child evolving in a particular framework evolving with a specific function. It is up to us to reveal the existing links between the behaviour of each member of the family. One of the richest aspects of intervention in the home resides in the possibility of foreseeing potential dangers in accordance with our perceptions of parental attitudes and the framework in which the family evolves.

It is evident that work in the surgery is sometimes as effective as sessions in the home, which is the reason why, in Geneva, there are also services for psychological follow-up such as infant guidance. However, certain nuances exist in our approach, nuances that are sometimes difficult for the parents to grasp but that allow the possibility of an alternative. Certain families will be more at home with one or other of these methods: the wider the range of possible interventions, the closer we will be to the welfare of the families.

An important preventive task is to advise on the different services available to the families who could make use of it. We sometimes effect brief interventions, in order to reassure the parents on the different stages that a child is entering in the course of his or her development and the repercussions that those stages can have on family equilibrium. Is it not preferable to inform, reassure, and advise these families asking for help rather than risk the slow collapse of some others?

Conclusion

The information available badly lacks studies on the real efficiency of intervention programmes in the homes of young children. Despite our conviction that we are carrying out work that is useful and necessary, the pressure of social insurance leads to questions of a financial nature linked to the cost-effectiveness of these follow-ups. One domain rarely escapes budget cuts: prevention. Unfortunately, we often notice afterwards that in the long term this has been a mistake. In fact, a house built on shaky foundations risks collapsing eventually, which is also true of the family unit.

Moreover, it has been proved that in the case of a child in difficulties, the sooner the intervention takes place, the better is the child's chance of evolving to his or her best potential.

The wide range of people with whom we intervene could allow us to measure the impact of intervention in the home, whether with regard to the handicap of the child or to the ability of the family to function.

CHAPTER EIGHT

Changing conversations

David Fourmy

> When new territories of therapeutic conversation are being
> entered into, it can take considerable time to become familiar
> with such territories and to become proficient in the skills
> associated with these explorations. The key is practice, practice
> and more practice . . . the expressions of life that seem most
> spontaneous to us are those that we have had the most
> practice in.
>
> Michael White (2007, p. 6)

This chapter focuses on the experience of a local multi-agency
team established in anticipation of government legislation
aimed at achieving better outcomes for children and young
people by ensuring all organizations and practitioners providing
services to children, such as schools, social workers, and health
professionals, worked together in a more effective way. During
the implementation and evaluation stages, the author was in the
role of project coordinator. Hopefully what was learnt over the life
of the project can be of value to practitioners working together in
other settings.

In their introduction to *Working Below The Surface: The Emotional Life of Contemporary Organizations* (Huffington, Armstrong, Halton, Hoyle, & Pooley, 2004), Armstrong and Huffington describe the impact on work contexts where increasingly there are "mergers, strategic alliances, and partnerships" and where internal structures and roles are "less clearly defined and conventional hierarchies less evidently relevant". They observed that very few practitioners "are unaffected by such change and the corresponding need to evolve new modes of adaptation, in the cause of survival and development, both individually and corporately" (p. 5).

It seems to be a common experience for professionals working in agencies that deliver services to children, young people, and their families to be confronted with a demand to "change" the way they work with each other within an organization, or across different services. No doubt this is "change for the better"; recipients are expected to receive a more effective response. But there are costs as well. For practitioners, particularly during a period of transition, there can be a sense of a "loss of professional identity", the experience of an erosion of claimed areas of specialism, and a belief that their service or agency is being led by new managers who lack an understanding of, and an appreciation for, their unique contribution. In a personal communication with the author, a practitioner from a service who had recently been placed in a locality team of "mixed professionals" expressed her feelings about the change she was experiencing: "I feel like I have lost the voice that was mine; even the meaning of the language of my specialism and my ways of working are being traded in for common words and processes; I feel more isolated now."

Change is, not infrequently, driven and managed through the imposition of new procedures that must be followed and new goals that are expected to be met, usually within a short time frame. There may be some attention to the need to support workers through a period of transition, but these measures (if any) are often under pressure from a set of corporate and agency objectives and from individual targets linked to large outcome measures, such as rates of school attendance, exclusion rates, and level of pupil attainment. There seems to be little emphasis on the kind of "bottom-up" processes that might help practitioners placed together from different agencies to "re-invent" themselves as a cohesive team through a process of supported group self-reflection.

Multi-agency working and the national context

Multi-agency working has developed rapidly in recent years in the United Kingdom in response to key legislation prompted by the Laming Report (Laming, 2003), which was triggered by the death of 8-year-old Victoria Climbié in February 2000 and is the most extensive inquiry in British history into the failings of the child protection system. Subsequently the Green Paper *Every Child Matters: Change for Children* (2003) set out the government's vision for children's services, and the Children Act 2004 underpinned the development of Children's Trusts, which are partnerships between different organizations that provide, commission, and deliver better outcomes for children and young people. More recent tragedies, notably the death of "Baby Peter", have emphasized the need for effective multi-agency working.

Traditionally, methods of working together between education, social care, healthcare, and community-based services have reflected either an approach where agencies have operated on an entirely separated basis, or through a loosely collaborative model, with some agreed arrangements for sharing information and for networking. This way of working has resulted in the kinds of gaps in provision and knowledge and significant deficiencies in inter-professional communication and multi-agency intervention that the Laming Report highlighted.

As a consequence of the Laming Report, government legislation has required changes in the way services work together at organizational and individual (practitioner) levels. New Children's Trust arrangements are designed to ensure that the "duty to cooperate" in the delivery of front-line integrated services is supported by strengthened inter-agency governance arrangements and by the adoption of a range of common processes, such as the use of a "Common Assessment Framework".

The government has argued that as well as ensuring earlier and more effective intervention for meeting the needs of vulnerable children and families, integrated working also provides benefits for professionals. It was anticipated that practitioners would gain a greater understanding of and respect for each other's contributions to achieving a clear understanding of issues and would feel more able to work together in both the assessment and the intervention phases. Multi-agency working would broaden each practitioner's approach to include a more holistic, richer picture of child and family needs and strengths. There are examples in the literature on multi-agency working that supports this view. Atkinson, Wilkin, Stott, Doherty, and Kinder (2002), writing about multi-agency work in school settings, described a number of positive outcomes of multi-agency working systems, including the development of enhanced or new working relationships, improved understanding or raised awareness of issues, and more effective ways of overcoming difficulties through "joined-up" thinking.

However, there is clear acknowledgement from the government that requirements for services to adopt new working styles, and undertake more "joined-up" work means that there will be a "significant cultural change" for everyone involved. In 2005 the Department for Education and Schools noted in their guidance for managers and practitioners that professionals "will be working with new people, with a new service remit and in a new way with children and families", adding that this would mean that "it will not be possible or appropriate to work in the same way they did before. It will probably mean abandoning, or at least reassessing, old assumptions, values and theories about how things work."

The GO Project

It was this "new way of working" that was being piloted in the GO Project. The project was undertaken over a two-year period from 2003 to 2005 within a small neighbourhood area in an Inner London local authority, with the overriding aim of improving the coordination and delivery of early intervention and support for children and young people, families, and schools.

The locality (referred to as the "GO" area, an abbreviation of the name of one of the communities within the area) was one of twenty Neighbourhood Pathfinder areas in London supported by the Neighbourhood Renewal Unit. The area was selected because of high levels of social deprivation and unemployment. The unemployment rate was 8.4%, nearly 2 percentage points above the local authority average of 6.6% and nearly 5 percentage points higher than the national average of 3.6% at that time. Unemployment among 16- to 19-year-olds was 10.9%: more than double the national average and 3.4 percentage points higher than the Camden average.

There were nearly 4,000 children aged between 0 and 14 years, and just over 5,000 young people aged between 15 and 29 years. Under-19-year-olds accounted for around one-third of the population, which was 12.5 percentage points above the borough average and 8.7 percentage points higher than the national average.

The establishment of a locality-based multi-agency team was the key initiative within the GO Project. The GO Multi-Agency Team (GOMAT) included practitioners from key agencies in education, health, and social services working collaboratively with other statutory and voluntary organizations providing services to the local community and to its twelve schools: one secondary school, seven primary schools, one special school, two secondary pupil referral units, and one nursery centre.

A baseline survey conducted in 2002 indicated that there was a need to provide better integrated service delivery in response to concerns identified by the community. Priorities identified included providing greater consultation with young people and their families, and swifter and easier access to agencies, with schools providing the local neighbourhood active "hubs" for engagement with services. Hence, a key project priority was to ensure that service providers worked together in a more effective way. This was to be achieved by locating the core members of GOMAT within a central school in the GO area and ensuring that arrangements were put in place for effective collaborative working with other practitioners from existing statutory and voluntary services, agencies, and teams. The scope of this work encompassed improving joint working and promoting a more "seamless" service that would enhance opportunities for children and young people; improve support for addressing concerns about pupil behaviour, truancy, and involvement in antisocial or criminal activity; enable better local access to services promoting the mental health and well-being of young people; and offer support for families at key transition stages (e.g., transfer from nursery to primary school).

The core project team consisted of a project coordinator, team manager (both part-time positions), an assistant clinical psychologist (primarily in a research and evaluation role), two parent and community officers, a social worker, and an administrative officer who was also responsible for publicity. Practitioners working in the GO area from Camden's Educational Psychology Service, as well as those in the Education Welfare Service and in the Safeguarding and Social Care Service, were seen as integral to the functioning of GOMAT.

Main services represented in GOMAT from the "core" and extended services

> Educational Psychology
> Social Services
> Educational Welfare
> Youth and Connexions
> Community Safety
> PLAY and Leisure services
> Child & Adolescent Mental Health Services
> Sure Start
> Youth Offending Team
> Housing.

The GO Project and its approach to multi-agency working

From the commencement of the project, it was clear to the team that creating a new system for services to work together would not only impact on key educational targets, but would also influence, and be influenced by, the dynamics, cultures, beliefs, and values of the individual components of that system. Each service representative brought different working practices, perceptions of other services, and ideas about how multi-agency work should be developed.

To provide a sound evidence base for GOMAT practice, a literature review on multi-agency working was undertaken prior to the commencement of the team's direct work. Although it is beyond the scope of this chapter to report the outcome of this review in detail, the key findings influencing the way GOMAT practitioners worked together will be considered here.

Evidence from the literature review highlighted some generally agreed key factors for ensuring that working together and managing change can be achieved:

> A shared vision of aims and objectives at all levels, and between agencies, defining common goals, and providing a focus on users' needs (Atkinson et al., 2002).

> Mutual understanding of expectations and constraints under which different agencies operate, in order to prevent misunderstandings and domination by one profession (Atkinson et al., 2002).

> Positive communication and information sharing, with clear protocols. Of particular interest to GOMAT was the conclusion that one-to-one human contact in an information-sharing system increased the frequency of communications, facilitated the development of respect and trust, and promoted the sharing of allocation and referral systems (Hudson, 2002).

> An effective engagement with service users. Developing relationships with, and finding ways to engage users can enhance quality of collaboration and improve outcomes for users (Townsley, Abbott, & Watson, 2004).

> An explicit attempt to address concerns about professional identity and anxiety about change. Examples include both personal and professional concerns about loss of professional identity (Spratley & Pietroni, 1994), role insecurity (Hudson, 2002), feelings of frustration, and disruption to existing work (Atkinson et al., 2002).

The literature review suggested that multi-agency working can be considered to be distinct from the traditional multidisciplinary information-sharing approach, which maintains separate systems of work. Lloyd, Stead, and Kendrick (2001) suggest that "inter-agency working" occurs when more than one agency work together in a planned and formal way, and that "joined-up" refers to deliberately conceptualized and coordinated planning and working that takes account of different policies and varying agency practices and values. McQuail and Pugh (1995, cited in Osgood & Sharp, 2000) identified three main organizational models: *collaborative* (agencies continue to work in separate departments), *integrated* (services brought together within a single department), and *coordinated* (separate agencies and services exist but work together within a formalized structure). Although "coordinated models" have often been considered to be just a step in the process towards full integration, McQuail and Pugh identified this model's particular value in appropriately meeting identified needs within a wider community area, without upsetting the equilibrium between authorities and local providers. A "coordinated" style of working can be thought of as the drawing together of a number of different agencies involved in the delivery of services so that there is a more coordinated and cohesive response to need.

In response to the literature review's main findings, the GO Project promoted a "coordinated", flexible working style, reflecting its focus on community work, as well as supporting existing multidisciplinary and multi-agency service delivery. A conscious decision was made to take the time necessary to think about and put into place the processes and procedures that seemed most likely to help practitioners embrace changes in practice. The literature reviewed on organizational change clearly identified that the informal "culture" of an organization (shared values and beliefs) can be a very powerful determinant of how people think and behave within it (Brunning, Cole, & Huffington, 1997). Furthermore, acknowledging cultural processes directly can be used as a form of "intelligence" to help manage and promote change (Huffington et al., 2004).

This understanding informed the early stages of development of the GO Project and was essential in addressing more fundamental resistances to cross-agency work, as well as helping to establish responsive networking. Key obstacles identified included local authority service managers not being sufficiently mindful of the principles and activities that were being promoted within the GO area, agency practitioners working part-time in the GO area continuing to orientate their style of practice on "home agency" perspectives and priorities, and schools holding unrealistic expectations of the range and depth of services that could be delivered through the new locally based (and hence much more visible) multi-agency team.

This foundation stage of the GO Project was also informed by a study on multi-agency work by Warmington et al. (2004), where the authors concluded that the acknowledgement of tensions and contradictions in multi-agency work is often overlooked in favour of promoting an ideal good-practice model. Difficulties such as these can impede the implementation of multi-agency work, and GOMAT's deliberate focus on a network-building function specifically addressed this potential barrier to change by encouraging the development of positive interactions and relationships throughout the service network. Of particular significance for GOMAT's evolvement was the view that the model of working was not as important as the degree to which different departments were able to work together (McQuail & Pugh, 1995, cited in Osgood & Sharp, 2000). This focus on creating an organizational climate that was characterized by positive interaction and cooperation, finds some support in a study by Glisson and Hemmelgarn (1998). In their examination of the effects of organizational characteristics on the quality and outcomes of children's service systems, they found that a positive organizational climate (characterized by low conflict, cooperation, role clarity, and personalization) was the primary predictor of service quality.

A decision was taken on the basis of these findings to design GOMAT meetings to be reflective forums that could provide a regular space for talking about current work with client groups, celebrating successes, and discussing any difficulties and anxieties about ongoing work and about professional roles. These weekly meetings, which were open to all practitioners from both the core and extended teams, enabled everyone present to work through practical and professional issues impacting on the delivery of services to children and families and affecting the achievement of the project's objectives. Through this open exchange of information and views, "secret" professional knowledge became the shared knowledge of professional collaboration. However, the purpose of the initial meetings was not simply information exchange; the aim was to provide a sense of "containment", which would enable practitioners to create together the kind of "significant cultural change" in working practices that was later highlighted in the *Every Child Matters* guidance. There was a sense of becoming a "narrative community" in these initial meetings, through the "telling and re-telling of stories", punctuated by expressions of curiosity, surprise, and shared enjoyment.

There was a planned gradual progression in the nature of these discussions, moving from an initial focus on general sharing of ideas, plans, and activities to meetings with increasing elements of peer consultation and group supervision of specific work raised by practitioners. It was not until a later stage in the development of the meeting process that the important function of providing a more formal case discussion, action, and review approach was included. This careful, reflective process set the foundation for effective joint working, as is exemplified in the case study described below.

Case study

The case described here demonstrates the benefits for an identified young child and her family of effective joined-up multi-agency working and also illustrates how the GO Project's focus on developing reflective, trusting, and respectful practices freed professionals to contribute their views and to take up the most appropriate and helpful roles in an agreed joint intervention.

The case was considered at a GOMAT meeting, with the discussion being led by a CAMHS clinician (a psychotherapist) who had developed a supportive relationship with the child's mother during sessions held within the child's school.

The family consisted of the identified child (a 6-year-old girl), the child's mother (pregnant with her third child), the child's father, and the mother's son (17 years old, whose father had been killed when he was 3 years old). Following the death of her husband, the boy and his mother migrated as refugees to London from Central Europe, and she later remarried, resulting in the birth of his half-sister.

The 6-year-old child had a Statement of Special Educational Needs (with the main area of additional need identified as "Language and Communication"). In her discussions with the child's mother, the CAMHS clinician recognized that there seemed now to be additional difficulties facing the child that had not been communicated to other professionals, and decided to bring the case to a GOMAT meeting.

To help frame the team's discussion, the common assessment framework was used to detail as richly as possible the child's and the family's needs and strengths and to gain a picture of the involvement and impact of services that had been working separately with the family over the last few years.

The child and family's identified additional needs included the following:

▹ The identified child's attendance at school had been falling, and her behaviour was increasingly withdrawn.

▹ There appeared to an enduring impact on the mother and her son's well-being, linked to unspecified trauma experiences in their home country.

▹ The 17-year-old boy had left school without any qualifications and was not in education, training, or employment.

▹ There were housing difficulties: the small, two-bedroomed flat meant that the 17-year-old had to share a bedroom with his 6-year-old sister.

▹ The mother expressed concerns about her son's relationship with his 6-year-old sister.

▹ There were relationship difficulties between parents, exacerbated by marked differences in parenting style.

▹ The mother suffered from long-term depression, which had been diagnosed by her doctor but had not been successfully treated with antidepressants.

▹ The parents were not engaging with a culturally focused voluntary agency that had offered support in the past.

Through a process of consultation the team decided that the CAMHS clinician was best placed to take on the lead professional role; she had developed a supportive relationship with the family and was in a good position to liaise with the school. An overall action plan involving a range of practitioners was devised to address the range of needs, with the CAMHS clinician taking the coordinating and family liaison role. This enabled the team to tackle:

- the child's educational difficulties through support from the GOMAT educational psychologist, in collaboration with the school's special educational needs coordinator and the speech and language therapist
- the mother's depression and coping with her pregnancy through GP involvement, a health visitor to provide antenatal support, and ongoing therapeutic support through a school-linked CAMHS clinician
- a family assessment regarding the brother's relationship with his sister to be completed by the GOMAT social worker
- parenting and relationship difficulties through re-establishing support for the family with a culturally appropriate voluntary agency
- attendance issues through the GOMAT education welfare officer liaising with the lead professional regarding strategies and support for the parents
- the son's unemployment through linking with voluntary organizations and Youth & Connexions to aid job search
- housing problems through reference to the Under 25s Centre manager to look at housing options for the son.

This example of "joined-up thinking and working" demonstrates how the right climate of engagement for practitioners can facilitate a well-prepared and well-planned multi-agency intervention, with the kind of effective, wide-ranging responses that are most likely to lead to the positive outcomes required by the *Every Child Matters* (DfES, 2004) agenda for practitioners to fulfil their "duty to cooperate".

Reflections and conclusions

A central part of GOMAT's work, especially initially, was the careful management of change for the members of the team by providing "a talking and thinking space". An underlying principle was the idea that it was important to develop a climate where there could be a rich exchange of views, freed from the constraints of professional roles, language, and anxieties and from the "oppression" of externally imposed tasks, chores, and targets. Indeed, in an independent review of the GO Project, it was noted that the project had "provided the space for professionals to learn from each other and undertake joint problem-solving and joint delivery of services to the community, schools and young people and their families" (Dickinson, 2005).

As part of the GO Project's own evaluation the team's assistant clinical psychologist, in her role as project researcher, interviewed practitioners individually, using semi-structured interviews (Breakwell, Hammond, & Fife-Schaw, 2000). Questionnaire data were analysed using descriptive statistics, with interview analysis based on Grounded Theory (Glaser & Strauss, 1967).

Feelings of professional efficacy, and learning from others, were associated in these interviews with overall positive views about the project and what it was trying to achieve. This has been associated in the literature on organizational change with increased motivation and with commitment to multi-agency work. What the analysis revealed was that the GO Project impacted on professionals by:

▸ providing opportunities to develop a clearer understanding of other services and to challenge negative perceptions of their own service

▸ enabling them to appreciate and integrate the views of other professionals into their casework

▸ promoting a sense of empowerment among professionals, enabling them to work more effectively in their changing roles, both with other professionals and with families in the GO area.

The following comments from GOMAT practitioners provide an illustration of the project's impact on their working practices in these three areas.

▷ *Increased awareness and understanding of how services operate*

"[GOMAT meetings] give services the opportunity to address any negative perceptions or misunderstandings about their work, and promote better understanding. . . . Meetings and training activities have introduced different perspectives and helped professionals to identify differences and similarities in the ways services work. This has helped to break down barriers in this forum and create a clearer understanding." *Youth Offending Team Worker*

"Close working with a clinical psychologist has helped to demystify the work of the other. More similarities than differences have been uncovered through this. Differences come mainly from the way in which services deploy their professional skills." *Educational Psychologist*

"My contact with GOMAT has extended my knowledge of other services." *Youth & Connexions Personal Adviser*

"[My involvement with GOMAT work] has impacted on the Youth Inclusion and Support Panel in a number of different ways including: Improving knowledge about the school system, providing a more rounded picture of young people, helping to develop an understanding of multi-agency working." *Youth & Connexions Manager*

▷ *Changing thinking and working culture*

"In discussing case examples, putting across your views and listening to the views of other professionals and the questions they ask in relation to cases introduces a different perspective." *Youth Offending Team Social Worker*

"[Successes of the project] challenge the way different agencies work and develop new ways of thinking around cases." *Youth & Connexions Manager*

"Meetings were useful in terms of getting a picture of the relatedness of services, and learning how services could link up. And also appreciating how everyone was in the same position—an experiential learning experience." *Educational Psychologist*

"You don't always need to assume that therapy is the answer, but that there may be other solutions in terms of linking with services in the community which meet different needs and may have a positive impact." *Clinical Psychologist*

> *Promoting efficacy, confidence, and empowerment*

"Meetings gave a sense of self as a professional and improved confidence in putting across professional views." *Youth Offending Team Worker*

"As an individual professional I have benefited from the advice given. Feedback [in a subsequent meeting], helped me realize how much work I'd done with that particular client." *Youth & Connexions Personal Adviser*

"Knowledge of local schemes . . . and familiarity with professionals working within these services also helped de-pathologise, and promote a link with the world of the client. This type of work is less threatening." *Clinical Psychologist*

"Meeting with, and developing professional relationships with, other people helps develop informal working networks which can in turn strengthen formal working networks." *Clinical Psychologist*

As has been noted earlier in this chapter, many factors contribute to successful multi-agency working, including clear but flexible and resilient leadership; a shared vision of aims and common, well-articulated goals; clear protocols and positive, open lines of communication; a mutual understanding of expectations and restraints; and a responsive awareness of the needs of users. These factors should not be undervalued. However, what the GO Project's findings have highlighted is the need for as great a commitment by services to positive ways of "being together" as there is to "working together" to meet even the most clearly articulated and shared aims and targets.

At its best, a "joined-up team" can be likened to a "learning community" whose members are well supported in the dynamic process of talking and thinking together, jointly shaping a climate that facilitates positive changes in practice. In his discussion of schools as learning communities, Fielding (1999) suggests that a "Community is a way of being, not a thing: [it] is a process through which human beings regard each other in a certain way . . . acting together in the mutuality as persons, not as role occupants" (p. 72). It is this sense of "being" in a working relationship with each other in a multi-agency team that can help make the difference when delivering a better service to vulnerable children, young people, and their families.

In conclusion, the GO Project has produced some understandings that the author hopes may be helpful for others who are either establishing multi-agency teams or who are beginning to "live" in them:

▷ There needs to be a good evidence-base for understanding what needs to be tackled and the management issues that will have to be addressed.

▷ The "bottom-up" contributions of reflective practitioners can more than complement "top-down"-driven approaches to developing integrated services to communities and schools; these are not mutually exclusive alternatives but equally valid approaches, and the interaction of the two needs to be skilfully managed to create the climate for optimum service delivery.

▷ The conscious and explicit provision of the psychological space (time, place, and processes) to help to develop and strengthen a positive teamwork climate is an important (and sometimes overlooked) factor in achieving good outcomes for children, young people, and their families.

▷ It takes planning and time for different professions to understand each other and for practitioners to have the conversations that help them to develop effective, different ways of being together.

By way of a postscript, the author would like to share the details of a recent discussion. It has been some years now since the conclusion of the GO Project, and by chance the author met one of the practitioners from the extended services group who had taken part in the GOMAT meetings. After some warm recollections, she said that now that the project had ended she "didn't do that kind of multi-agency working any more" and felt "quite disconnected" from other agencies and services working in the local community; in this sense she had been rendered "speechless" again. This was a salutary reminder to the author that emerging narratives can be fragile. Our new conversations need time to nourish the growth of the change we seek.

Acknowledgements

The author would like to acknowledge the work of Claire Russon, Assistant Clinical Psychologist during the GO Project, whose valuable contribution to the review of literature on multi-agency working helped to provide the evidence base for the team's work; excerpts from Claire's interviews with team members are also quoted in this chapter. The author would also like to thank Sadegh Nashat, Senior Consultant Clinical Psychologist, for his essential contribution to the success of the project through his role as GOMAT Manager.

CHAPTER NINE

"Fox's Earth": developing social links in a traumatized community

Simonetta Adamo

In this chapter, I describe a project that took place in a nursery school in an impoverished district of Naples in southern Italy. This was an extremely deprived area characterized by high levels of poverty, unemployment, and social breakdown, where drug trafficking and organized crime [*camorra*] were rife. In the period immediately prior to the project, a "war" had erupted between various gangs in the area, resulting in a number of deaths in the local community. Seeking to do something about the climate of terror that prevailed, a group of teachers and heads of local nursery schools approached the city council's "Early Years" service. The university where I am employed became involved, and "Fox's Earth"—a project that took place over three years—was born.

The principal idea was to offer children, families, and teachers the experience of a stable, safe space in which ordinary, everyday activities—play, conversation, meetings—could be re-established in a climate of care, understanding, and shared concern for life.

In the first section of this chapter, I describe the context—how the project was structured, the characteristics of the staff group, and the nature of the activities offered. I also focus on the work that went into staff training, which included a fortnightly supervision seminar. This seminar, which I led, was based on the method of infant observation originally conceived by Esther Bick (1964) and subsequently developed at the Tavistock Clinic in the training of child psychotherapists and other professionals involved in work with children. The way in which the method was adapted to suit the particular context of the project is also be briefly discussed.

Lastly, I give some clinical examples in order to illustrate more vividly the reflective process the supervision seminar sought to develop.

The "Fox's Earth" Project

"Fox's Earth" was an experimental project that developed out of a collaboration between Naples City Council's "Early Years" service and the Federico II University. Funding was provided by a local foundation for children's welfare. The project was designed for children, parents, and nursery teachers living and working in Scampia, a highly deprived district of the city of Naples.

In 2004, when the project began, Scampia had been devastated by a war waged by local gangs for control of the drugs market. The deaths of a number of innocent people had caused widespread public terror and revulsion. Numerous families had already left the neighbourhood. Many more were considering moving, and those that remained were often too frightened to send their children to school. Instead, they sought refuge at home from a climate of hate, fear, and suspicion.

When a group of local teachers and heads of nursery schools contacted the city council's "Early Years" service, requesting a meeting to discuss a possible intervention, the university's Clinical Psychology and Applied Psychoanalysis Unit became involved, thanks to its long history of collaborating with local authorities on projects promoting child & adolescent mental health in educational settings (Adamo, Adamo Serpieri, Giusti, & Tamajo Contarini, 2008; Adamo & Aiello, 2006).

The request

It is important to emphasize at this point that the request for intervention originated from the schools, since this demonstrates—like all requests for help—the existence of a basic trust that some response would be forthcoming. A silence, by contrast, may not indicate the absence of need but a mute, frustrated expectation, a lack of any hope of a response.

I would also like to stress the quality of the teachers' request— not a claim or a demand, but the expression of a feeling of co-responsibility, a wish for partnership. It was not an order to "Do something!" or worse a complaint—"Why do you do nothing?"— but, rather, an appeal: "Let's do something; let's do it quickly, and let's do it together!"

This quality of co-responsibility formed the basis of a shared planning, which began with the selection of the school that would become the project's base. Typically this is the phase in a project in which tensions can easily surface as different parties seek to control or to else try distance themselves in order to avoid further burdens and responsibilities. In this case, however, the search for a base was dictated by a shared wish to find somewhere that the project could flourish. The location of the school, for instance, was extremely important. Since the activities of the project would take place during the late afternoon, it was vital that the location was a central one. This was, after all, a time when families were reluctant to venture outside, when both the perception and the reality was that the streets were unsafe. A convenient, accessible location was therefore crucial. Child psychotherapist Cathy Urwin (2003) describes the birth of a similar project based in a neighbourhood in London characterized by "particularly high levels of deprivation and ethnic diversity" and aimed at giving support to families with young children. Urwin stresses the importance of finding sites that were "within buggy-pushing distance"—in other words, sites that could be easily reached by parents, taking into account the needs of families with babies and young children.

Security was another crucial issue. I was given a very powerful sense of what teaching in Scampia involved when I was matter-of-factly informed that one particular school, which in many ways seemed suitable, could not be used because it was close to a park where drug users regularly gathered. Teachers at this school, I was told, had painted the window panes in order to protect the children from the sight of what went on outside.

Another consideration in the choice of school was the need to find workers willing to commit themselves to the project. The motivation of teachers and other professionals has been crucial to its success. Not only did they act as intermediaries between the planners and the families, they also helped to overcome unavoidable organizational and bureaucratic difficulties. Most importantly of all, they took an active part in the project, which was specifically designed around them.

The context

The ongoing violence that was devastating the area took place against a background of chronic problems. The district of Scampia had been built in the early 1970s as part of a State programme of low-cost social housing. In fact, the district was never completed. Basic infrastructures, services, squares, leisure, and sports facilities are still missing; levels of unemployment and school truancy are high, and the presence of organized crime is strong and pervasive. There are many single-parent families as well as high levels of poverty and deprivation; many families struggle with drug use and/or mental health problems. The whole population is acutely affected by the general decay and insecurity of the area and from strongly held prejudices towards its inhabitants.

At the point at which the project was conceived, there was the additional problem of excessive media attention, which often served to reinforce stereotypes about the area and to exploit personal tragedies.

The project's aim

Working in Scampia has meant, especially in the early stages of the project, working with a population that was facing actual trauma. The aim was not to provide a therapeutic space for working through this experience; instead, we sought to offer an intervention that would re-establish, as far as was possible, everyday, ordinary ways of life in order to help individuals to regain contact with situations, feelings, and parts of themselves that were free from traumatization. In the first instance, what was felt necessary was not to create opportunities to speak about the actual "emergency" but, instead, to facilitate the space for experiences and relationships which would re-assert values that had been violated. By offering a calm, continuous, and predictable environment and by providing relationships that modelled qualities of thoughtfulness, care, and protectiveness towards the youngest and most vulnerable members of the community, it was hoped that growth could be encouraged.

Naming the project

One of the first considerations in choosing a name for the project was therefore the idea of creating a refuge, a protected space. However, this was not the only objective. In terms of its architecture and toponymy, the borough of Scampia is marked by anonymity. Even the nursery schools have no names of their own but are merely called after the streets on which they are located. Once again, this absence of identity is paradoxically reinforced by the excessive visibility of the borough in the media. The whole district is, in fact, shrouded in a negative identity, which compounds its sense of loss of individuality. Choosing a name for the project was therefore deeply significant.

Eventually the name "Fox's Earth" emerged from a number of associations, both to the school that was to host the project, where a heap of earth in the garden was believed to be a fox's den, and to the infantile meaning of the "den" as a safe, protected space. In this case, however, the meaning was not limited to a place where families retreat out of fear, but was extended to encompass a welcoming social, collective space. The sense of the den, the shelter—the earth—could be achieved by recognizing oneself as being in a shared identity, in a pact of joint responsibility which linked families and institutions, in a community based on the care of new generations.

In children's literature, it is interesting to note that the character of the fox figures in *Le Petit Prince* (1943) by Antoine de Saint-Exupéry. The fox teaches the little prince that it is the creation and acknowledgement of intimate links that makes individuals and relationships unique.

At a party celebrating the end of the first year of the project's work, a little boy pulled at the sleeve of one of the workers and asked her: "But 'Earth' isn't finished, is it? 'Earth' just goes on holidays, doesn't it?" What this child's question conveyed was that "Earth" had become a way of being together, a shared space with its own times, rules, and rituals, with a culture of its own.

The identity of the project was reinforced by the creation of a logo that was put on all communications with families—from the initial letter that announced the welcome party at which representatives from the different institutions involved, together with staff members, described the project to the invited families, to the list of participants that was later drawn up by the school's head. As the first year of activities drew to an end and no one was certain about whether or not we could continue, we seized on the idea that the meaning of the project could endure, even after its actual conclusion. We decided to give all the participants—parents, teachers, children—a certificate of attendance. In addition, we gave all the children a T-shirt with the name and logo of the project. Continuity, stability, and predictability have characterized the project since its inception and have allowed the possibility that, despite its short duration, it had a meaningful impact.

The structure of the intervention

The project lasted for three years. During this time it underwent numerous changes in order to better meet different needs and to respond to difficulties. In this section, I focus on the first year of activities, which took place on a weekly basis over a five-month period.

Every Wednesday the school remained open for two hours after the end of the normal school day in order to host the project's activities. At the beginning of each meeting, thirty minutes were reserved for an introductory welcome for families who were arriving and for the children who were finishing their school day. This was a time when all workers—teachers, families, project staff—gathered together and where informal communication could take place in a relaxed atmosphere. An afternoon snack—milk, homemade biscuits, or cake—was offered. Following this, children, parents, and teachers went on to their separate activities. Parents took part in a group led by two psychologists in which they were encouraged to share and to discuss parenting issues. Those who wanted to discuss problems more privately were offered individual counselling sessions with another psychologist.

Meanwhile, the children were divided into three groups according to age and went off to different activities. The "play workshop" and the "storytelling workshop" were aimed at 2- to 6-year-old children, while the workshop for the "older siblings" was for 7- to 13-year-olds.

The first workshop was led by two play leaders who facilitated, accompanied, and supervised the children's free play. The storytelling workshop was run by a school teacher alongside a youth worker and was divided into three stages: first the children were told a story, and then they were invited to draw it and, finally, to dramatize it.

The "older siblings" workshop was run by two workers and concentrated on music. The children were given the opportunity to listen to music and to play it, with instruments that they had made. In all the workshops, an observer was present. The observations were gathered and used as the basis for discussion in the supervision seminar, which I discuss later.

Finally, the nursery school teachers took part in a workshop based around the creative recycling of waste materials. This workshop, entitled "King Midas" after the king who, in Greek mythology, transformed everything he touched into gold, aimed to familiarize the teachers with the work that had taken place in another project initiated by the city council's "Early Years" service. Although this project had been open to children and their teachers from local schools, the climate of isolation and emotional deprivation meant that most teachers working in the Scampia district had not attended. The "King Midas" project was therefore designed to reach out to them, in the hope that first-hand experience would encourage them to attend subsequent workshops with their pupils.

Two members of staff from the earlier project joined the "Fox's Earth" team to lead a weekly workshop for teachers and to take part in the supervision seminars.

The staff

The project's staff team was made up of teachers, youth workers, psychology trainees, clinical psychologists, and child psychotherapists. Their ages and levels of practical experience and formal qualification varied considerably, ranging from young people with no academic qualifications to recent graduates and senior professionals. This range of experience lent richness to the project and contributed to the sense of a multi-generational, supportive, and professional community. Some of the younger workers, for instance, with no academic qualifications, were recruited because of their experience of voluntary work with marginalized families in the borough. They were, in fact, highly "qualified" by their practical experience. On the other hand, the psychology trainees who participated in the project as part of a one-year postgraduate training were keen to put their academic theory into practice. Their role in the project was to carry out observations of all the activities that took place, and their contribution was therefore particularly useful.

Over all, the youthfulness of the staff—their idealism, energy, and enthusiasm—proved to be invaluable. These qualities would regularly reinvigorate worn-out parents, teachers, and senior staff members. The senior members of the team helped to stabilize the group and to maintain a sense of direction and perspective.

The supervision

A key aspect of the project was the supervision seminar. All the staff, a total of eighteen people, met fortnightly for two and a half hours at the university. Each seminar was run by two professionals and involved a psychologist as observer. This pairing of professionals performed several functions in a way that bears many similarities to professional pairings in other settings—for example, in family therapy and the experience of co-leadership offered by the course for teachers and professionals involved in education at the Tavistock Clinic (Hartland-Rowe, 2005).

In our case, the experience of a creative and mutually supportive exchange was, I think, especially fruitful for the staff, because it counteracted powerful feelings of isolation and fragmentation stirred up by work with families who were often fragmented themselves as well as isolated from other families and from the wider community. It helped them to have an experience of the reflective work and concern of a parental couple. At a symbolic level, the couple relationship was between the feelings and the dynamics observed in the work and its organizational and institutional aspects. This, of course, often included the necessity of facing the frustration evoked by the absence of an ideal, wished-for relationship.

In a seminal paper entitled "The Old Lady Who Lived in a Shoe" (1981), child psychotherapist Shirley Hoxter uses the well-known nursery rhyme to explore "the state of mutual persecution" that can dominate the relationship between teachers and pupils in a school where adequate containment cannot be provided. Hoxter applies Bion's (1970) ideas to describe how the benign or pathological quality of the containing relationship can affect the well-being of both children and teachers, as well as the school as a whole. However, it is very important, writes Hoxter, that mental health professionals working in the school have the opportunity to understand the legal, economic, and political limitations that have caused the authorities to provide such an unsuitable container—the collapsed and worn-out shoe—to teachers and professionals working in an educational context.

In the "Fox's Earth" Project, establishing a time and a setting in which these kinds of issues could be confronted and discussed with a representative of the institution—the city council—proved enormously helpful in reducing the resentment towards the authorities that work within a very difficult context can easily engender. It reduced the risk that destructive dynamics would paralyse the group's work, leading to a blaming of the families, the teachers, or the authorities.

The discussions in the supervision seminar were based on detailed observation taken during the different activities. In all cases (with the exception of the counselling setting and the recycling workshop) the interactions were recorded by psychology trainees who did not actively take part in the work and were therefore non-participant observers. The psychology trainees received initial instruction in the observation's methodology. According to the method of infant observation originally developed by Esther Bick, they were instructed not to use technological equipment but to record, in detail, the verbal and nonverbal interactions they observed, seeking to avoid premature judgement or interpretation. Given the specific context, however, some differences were introduced. For example, in the case of the play and storytelling workshops, the children were between 3 and 6 years old. This was therefore essentially a young-child observation that confronted the observer and the group, with all the particularities and adjustments that observing children of this age requires (Adamo & Rustin, 2001), starting with a re-consideration of the meaning of the "neutrality" of the observer.

Another area where differences were introduced was in the timescale of the observation. Each workshop lasted an hour and a half, and this phase of the project continued for only five months. The duration of each single observation was therefore longer than the usual hour, while the span of the observation as a whole was considerably shorter than the traditional one-year period. A further difference was the focus of the observations. Observers were instructed not to focus upon a single child (as would be the case in young-child observation), but to provide a more general observation of the group of children (which varied in number from six to twelve) and of the relationships between them and with the workers. In fact, the method adopted could be located halfway between the more traditional approach followed in young-child observation and the observation of institutions, as described by Hinshelwood and Skogstad (2000).

In the cases of the counselling setting and the workshop with the teachers, the presence of an observer was felt to be inappropriate and observations were therefore carried out by the professionals themselves. Here the use of observation was more similar to the experience of professionals who attend work discussion seminars in Tavistock-model courses (Rustin & Bradley, 2008). In both methods, however, the aim of the seminar was to encourage reflection and a questioning attitude, to seek out links, and to pay attention to small but meaningful variations in seemingly repetitive behaviours, with a particular focus on the interrelation between the educational and the psychological aspects of the interactions.

A second seminar took place on a fortnightly basis and was organized by the city council's "Early Years" service. The main task of this seminar was the discussion of organizational issues, with an eye on both the outer reality (rules, roles, finances, etc) and the underlying dynamics.

Clinical examples

I would now like to give some clinical examples in order to better describe the methodology and to illustrate more vividly some of the work undertaken. Three shorter vignettes are followed by a more detailed case.

A ship sailing in the night

The first example illustrates the way in which a psychoanalytic perspective was used to explore interactions that took place within the educational setting. This double perspective is enriching, since it opens the mind to the complexity, density, and multi-layered meanings of the learning relationship. The following vignette is an excerpt from a presentation given by one of leaders of the workshop for teachers on creative recycling.

In one of her observations, the workshop leader described how a nursery teacher had commented on an object that she had made: "It was supposed to be a Christmas tree, but instead it has become a ship sailing on the sea in the night. . . ." It was noted by the group that the teacher was probably also referring to her expectations about the workshop. Perhaps when she had started she had expected to receive some ready-made "educational object"—a technique or piece of advice that she could easily apply to her own work with children. Her comment seemed to hint at an understanding that what the workshop could offer her instead was the experience of a journey where she needed to leave what was already known and to accept the uncertainty that is a part of true learning.

The consequences of a trauma

The second example concerns a 4-year-old boy, whom I will call Giulio. Giulio was quickly introduced by the nursery teachers to the psychologists as a "boy who had had a very serious car accident and who had awoken after a long period in a coma". The accident seemed to have left its mark not only on the boy's body but on his personality and relationships. In fact, Giulio could no longer separate from his mother and was very controlling and possessive towards her. The presence at the supervision seminar of all the professionals involved with Giulio and his family, together with the opportunity to gather together observations from different settings, made it possible to make a number of different interventions.

In the counselling sessions, it was possible to discuss with the mother how the real problem affecting Giulio was not so much the disability he was left with as a result of the accident, but what Valerie Sinason (1992) has called the "secondary handicap"—the psychological consequences resulting from the accident which had superimposed themselves upon it. Giulio had been apart from his mother when he had been hit by the car. Separation had subsequently become impossible for the mother–child couple since both feared that this could leave the child dangerously exposed to terrible consequences. Another issue that was discussed was how difficult it seemed for these parents, who had seen their son come very close to death, to set any limits for him. As a result he had become extremely tyrannical in his attempts to reclaim his mother as his exclusive possession.

The work with the psychologist helped Giulio's mother to become more aware of these dynamics and more aware of her need to embark on a longer period of psychological work. She accepted a referral to another service within the Italian National Health Service where she was offered psychotherapeutic treatment.

In the play workshop, it was possible to observe how Giulio attempted to establish a similar exclusive and controlling relationship with the workshop leader. Melanie Klein (1924) noted that the child experiences towards the teacher and his classmates at school the same feelings he originally had about his mother and siblings. In this case, because these figures were not the same as Giulio's primary love objects, a modification of the original feelings was made possible, allowing changes to the rigidity of repetitive patterns. Once the underlying dynamics were understood, the workshop leader felt more able to resist Giulio's controlling behaviour, and it then became possible to observe changes. On one occasion, Giulio "played" a game with another child, pretending that the workshop leader was a prisoner who had to be tied up. Here he was able to give symbolic representation, in shared play, to his desire for total control, a desire that is common to all children but which, in Giulio's case had not been met with the necessary, gradual disillusionment.

Death as spectacle

The third example comes from the discussion group with parents. In a session towards the end of the first year, the parents began to discuss a recent *camorra* ambush that had caused the death of three youngsters not far from the nursery school. By this point it had become possible for the parents in the group to share their deep feelings about the situation in the community, and tension in the room was high. Some of the mothers cried. One said that she had watched everything that had happened after the ambush from the balcony of her house. Her child had been watching beside her. At a certain point, the mother reported, the child had left her and had disappeared into his grandparents' room. She had discovered him hiding in the corner between two pieces of furniture.

Towards the end of the project, the parents seemed to have gained the necessary distance and trust that allowed them to share extremely painful feelings with the group. On this occasion, it was also possible to discuss how the child seemed to have been searching in his grandparents' room for a safe mental space that he had been unable to find with his mother, who was probably too bound up with the traumatic situation. "These children", writes Margaret Rustin (2005),

> represent the hopes of the city's future, but we know that parents with young children are acutely vulnerable to being overwhelmed by the intensity of the responsibility of caring for young lives. Unless they are provided with support and have a sense of basic security, parents' capacity to protect and encourage their children's development is easily undermined. The young families in the unsafe areas of the city are profoundly at risk.

This mother's capacity to protect her child, already fragile due to socioeconomic and cultural deprivation, was further undermined by her state of actual trauma, which caused her to lose sight of the need to protect a child from voyeuristic exposure to violent death.

The child who wanted to be Flash

My last example concerns a little boy, Pietro, who participated in the project for a two-year period. This case will therefore allow us to consider some of the significant changes that took place over this time.

Pietro was 5 years old when we first met him. The following observations were taken at the beginning of the first year and at the end of the second year.

First observation, first year

Pietro is a slim child with a pleasant face and a serious expression. He introduces himself as Flash and does not answer when he is addressed as Pietro, repeating that his name is Flash. He spends his entire time running around the room where the workshop takes place, "running faster than light" and resisting any attempt by the adults to make him sit down with the other children. On several occasions he even tries to leave the play workshop and to enter the room of the storytelling workshop in which his older sister is taking part.

Final observation, second year

The two workshop leaders have brought with them a big box that is attracting the children's curiosity. It is the shape of a television but made of cardboard. One of the leaders begins to turn a wooden stick on the top of the box, and a series of images start to appear. . . . These are children's drawing about the story they have been working on over the last few months. After a few moments, during which the children appear to be surprised and puzzled by the images that are being shown in turn, several voices start to pipe up: "but that's mine!"; "I made that!" The workshop leaders involve the children in the reconstruction of the story and ask them about what might be added to it. Eventually the children suggest that they could do some drawings about what happens next in the story. While one of the workshop leaders, a woman, distributes pens, the other, a man, places the box in a cupboard and lays out sheets of paper on the floor. Pietro follows him and tells him: "This story is beautiful, isn't it? It is really beautiful . . ." When the workshop leader asks him what he would like to draw, Pietro replies that he wants to draw a superhero. The workshop leader suggests that he might draw Guizzino (a little fish who is the main character in the story the children have been told). Guizzino, he explains, is like a superhero. "Nooo!", exclaims Pietro, "I will draw a shark."

There is a striking contrast between these two images: the little boy "running faster than light" described in the first vignette and captured in most of the observations of the first year, and the little child who follows step by step behind the adult, rather like the famous ethnologist Konrad Lorenz's little ducks. But if we return to the observations that took place in between and look closely at the detail (as we did in the supervision seminar), it is possible to trace a gradual development.

In one of the workshops, a few weeks after the beginning of the work, the observer writes:

At the end of the meeting, Pietro stops running for a second. A member of staff wonders aloud about whether Flash has to run so fast in order to escape from something. . . . Pietro smiles. "Yes", he says, and sets off again around the room. . . . A bit later, as he is speeding about, he begins to taunt the workers, shouting: "Come and get me." To his great amusement, he is chased and caught.

This sequence is repeated, with a few variations, in the following observation:

Pietro lies on the carpet, and, after covering himself with cushions, initially says: "I am not here!" After a while, he exclaims: "Find me!"

It is very interesting to see how the staff member's comment about Flash's need to run in order to escape a danger seems to have brought about a change in Pietro's behaviour. The little child who sought to avoid the workers' arms, creating a situation where the only contact could be a kind of claustrophobic and paralysing trap, now seems to experience the staff member's words, and the understanding that they convey, as a pleasurable and desired link. We could imagine that this development also took place because, when referring to Flash's need to escape, the staff member was very careful both in the timing and in referring to Flash rather than directly to the child. This reminds us of the importance, emphasized by the educational psychologist Mia Beaumont (1991), of "staying with the metaphor" when working with children in schools. The metaphor could either be the reference to a cartoon character, as in the case of Flash, or to a play, as in the case described by Beaumont.

In the last workshop of the first year, when, because of the anxieties stirred up by the imminent ending, Pietro probably feels more vulnerable, he communicates more clearly how his identification with Flash helps him to defend himself against contact with more fragile aspects of himself:

Pietro tries to enter a small tent where another child is hiding. The boy gives him a little slap. Pietro begins to shout: "I am going to hit you! . . ." A worker tries to calm him down by talking to him, but the boy is unrestrainable. She picks him up to stop him, but he kicks out, trying to escape and shouting to the other boy: "You are a little shit; I am going to beat you up; I am Flash!" Another worker intervenes and tells Pietro that it is enough and he is to stop. "I am not Pietro, I am Flash!" "No," says the worker. "You are Pietro and you've got to be still." The child looks at her and replies: "If I am Pietro, I want to go to my mummy!"

In the observations of the second year, we learn that Pietro assumes multiple identities. Sometimes he is Superman, sometimes Spiderman, sometimes Peter Pan. However it is interesting to note that he is no longer Pietro-Flash; in the observer's notes, he has become just Pietro. This change seems linked to the fact that a variety of different behaviours have begun to appear. Instead of running out of the room, he announces that he is going. He heads for the door, puts his hand on the handle, but then gives up and finds a place under the table from where he watches the other children playing. From here developments, can take place as is clear in the following observations.

Pietro assumes his corner under the table and is joined there by another child. Together, they watch the other children playing and then join them.

Pietro starts to bring with him a toy that represents a superhero and to play with it. During one workshop, he takes a family of dolls, selects the grandparents, and puts them carefully on the table as if they are meant to watch. He then takes the superhero toy and makes him fly around in front of the grandparents.

While it is not possible here to explore the detail of these interesting observations, they seem to suggest that little Pietro has gradually been able to let go of his omnipotent identification with a superhero and, simultaneously, to become more able to remain in the room, to concentrate, to get involved in play, either alone or with other children, and to use symbolic play. In the last sequence, for instance, he seems to acknowledge the others, but what is even more significant is the way he shows that play can take place in the presence of interested and benevolent adults. A real "capacity to be alone", as Winnicott (1958) has described, can only develop against the background of the silent, benevolent mother's presence.

The benevolent, silent presence that Pietro portrays in his play is also perhaps that of the observer, a presence that leaves him free to run about without losing the attention of an adult. When, in fact, he runs out of the storytelling workshop, he then reappears in the notes of the observer in the play workshop! So, in a sense, when he runs out of the room and escapes the attention of the adults in charge of him, he "falls" into the attention of other adults. I stress this because I have often thought how easily Pietro could have fallen into the diagnostic category of hyperactive children and perhaps have been given medication. I want to suggest that, in his case, it was the closely woven net of professionals around him sharing observations and reflections that seemed to have provided him with a safe holding.

But what about his need to escape, so acutely perceived by the worker? This can be more easily understood in the light of some information about his family situation. Both his sister, who was 7 years old, and his mother attended the project, and his mother requested individual counselling. Pietro's mother seemed to be very preoccupied by her relationships with her own father and with her husband, and in her counselling sessions she understood how much her anxieties about her role as daughter and as wife were interfering with her maternal functioning, resulting in her discharging her disowned feelings, among them anger, onto her children. Very interestingly, mother was able to gain some aware-ness of these dynamics, as can be seen in a comment she once made while observing Pietro's frantic movements: "Could it be that he is running away from our constant family quarrels?"

It is noteworthy that the staff team's picture of the family's mental heath was very different from the one held by the family and the school. While Pietro was considered "the problem" and his sister the "good one", our observations allowed us to hypothesize a very different situation. I think, in fact, that Pietro's running was an adaptive defence against the risk of being used by his mother as a "receptacle" for her unacceptable feelings, while his strong identification with a superhero probably provided him with the protection and reassurance that he could not find in his too-over-whelmed mother. Gianna Williams (1997) suggests that this may be the case in a developmental situation where instead of the mother acting as a "container" for her infant's disturbing feelings, she uses her infant as a "receptacle" in which to evacuate her own undigested anxieties.

In the case of Pietro's sister, both the mother's comments and the notes from the observations contributed to a picture of a girl who was trapped in a situation where she masochistically complied with her mother's unhealthy use of her. Her personality structure seemed to be dominated by something very compliant that pushed her to appear as a pseudo-adult figure who disavowed all childishness and who projected any vulnerability and neediness into the "little ones".

In this case, therefore, the intervention offered by the project contributed to an understanding of Pietro's separation anxiety and helped to facilitate some growth. It also helped to gather a more general overview of the family dynamics and to assess both the previously unnoticed pathological aspects of his sister's personality and her need for further help.

Concluding remarks

By way of concluding my account of our Neapolitan project, I would like to quote from Margaret Rustin's (2005) description of "Fox's Earth":

> There is a combination of commitment and seriousness on the one hand, and imagination and playfulness on the other, in the approach of the professionals involved. . . . The developments have depended on building links that one would not have expected. The university, with its access to skilled professionals, and city and community leaders in the educational and wider political context, have joined up to explore initiatives in the deprived and socially excluded parts of the city. Different layers of the city's resources and difficulties are connected through

innovative structures. This heterogeneity goes beyond what we usually mean by multidisciplinary approaches. It is important that there is a multigenerational mix both in the project workers and those whose lives they hope to improve—children, adolescents, parents, grandparents. . . .

The possibility of regenerating dilapidated areas is not simply one of restoring what might be considered the more harmonious and containing structures of the past, but of creating something new which is a genuine response to current circumstances. These kinds of projects depend for their health on discoveries, the possibility of surprises, inventiveness. There is a desire to prevent a despairing repetition of the experience of previous generations—to interrupt the cycle of intergenerational trauma—and this is only going to be achieved by finding a new outcome. We see play as the natural creative expression of children, and there needs to be an equivalent in the practice of professional work. Creativity in work reinvigorates the hopefulness, interest and sustainability of the efforts required of the adults in difficult circumstances. . . . To take this seriously requires building in time for reflection and professional discussion and evaluation. Unless these projects are not only conceived but also tended very carefully (like new plants in the garden) they will not flourish.

These words beautifully describe the challenge of "Fox's Earth", and of similar projects, that under different skies unite professionals committed to creating conditions in which the full potential of an educational experience can flourish, promoting in a meaningful way the growth of children, families, and professionals alike.

Acknowledgements

I would like to thank Flavia Portanova, head of Naples City Council's "Early Years" service, who co-planned the project with me and the "Fondazione Banco di Napoli per l'assistenza all'infanzia e all'adolescenza" who funded it. A special thank you to Margaret and Michael Rustin for the constant support and inspiration they give me.

CHAPTER TEN

The role of a child & adolescent mental health service with looked-after children in an educational context

Rita Harris & Yvonne Ayo

In the chapter we apply ideas from systemic and attachment theories to the needs of looked-after children and young people within an educational context. We draw on our expertise of working with this population within schools.

Children and young people placed away from their birth families, whether in long-term foster placements or adopted, have significant and varied emotional and psychological needs. This is also true of those who care for these children and young people and is now reflected in recent political and policy developments focusing on the needs of these children and families. However, in our experience, little has been available to practitioners in education to understand and meet the particular needs of these children and their carers.

Studies that have looked at the state of child mental health in Great Britain in both the general population and in looked-after children and young people have demonstrated worrying levels of mental health disorder in general. Recent statistics (Meltzel, Gatward, Curbin, Goodman, & Ford, 2003) show that the overall rate of diagnosable mental health disorder in looked-after young people up to 17 years of age in England and Wales is 45%: 37%

of these had clinically significant conduct disorders; 12% were assessed as having emotional disorders, anxiety, and depression; and 7% were diagnosed as hyperactive. Of the children and young people in residential care, 72% had a mental health disorder, 60% with a conduct disorder; this is perhaps not surprising as the most disturbed and disturbing young people are likely to find themselves in residential care. Those in kinship care have a lower rate of disturbance, 33%. The prevalence of childhood mental health disorders tended to decrease with the length of stay in the current placement, from 49% of those in their first year of placement to 31% in their fifth year.

The home–school relationship can be particularly problematic between the care and education systems. Frequent placement changes and high rates of exclusion mean that children in care are five times more likely than other children to move school in Years 10 and 11, a major factor affecting examination performance: 27% of children in care have a statement of special educational needs.

Research indicates that foster-carers often attribute little importance to schooling and that schools often fail to understand the needs of children in care (*Care Matters*, DfES, 2006a, p. 18). Exclusions from school are also a major issue for children in the care system. Some 0.9% of children in care were permanently excluded in 2004/05, compared with 0.1% of all children. Of the young people, 62% were one or more years behind with their schooling. Not only do children and young people in care have poor mental and physical health, they also do less well than their peers when leaving care. As reported in 1997, only 25% of care leavers had any academic qualifications; 50% were unemployed; 17% of young women were pregnant/were already mothers (DFES, 1997); and 20% were homeless within two years of leaving care (Biehal, Clayden, Stein, & Wade, 1995).

The impact of early adversity, multiple placements, and professionals' limited understanding of their mental health needs can result in behaviours that are difficult to understand and manage and can have long-term effects. Although crucial, simply offering opportunities and high levels of care are often not sufficient to enable children and young people to access the opportunities they are provided with.

Recent research has shown that early experiences, such as

trauma, have long-term impact on a child's ability to concentrate; difficulties in taking new information and learning; heightened sense of threat; and difficult behaviour. Trauma may include physical and emotional neglect and abuse, exposure to violent acts such as domestic violence, adult self-harm and sudden death, and all the traumatic situations that refugees and asylum seekers face and have experienced.

Neglect and the lack of good experiences can lead to the lack of development of confidence and self-esteem, leading to withdrawal and difficulties with peer groups in home life and learning. Children who have inconsistent and changeable care can develop controlling and defensive strategies (Glaser & Prior, 2006), which means they struggle to trust new carers and also struggle to learn or to trust their teachers. In addition, recent research has shown that the resulting behaviour can be experienced by education staff as frustrating and difficult to understand.

Policy framework

Given the high vulnerability and the recognition of the long-term needs of this group they have become a major priority for government policy makers as evidenced in *Care Matters* (DfES, 2006a) and *Every Child Matters* (DfES, 2004).

The White Paper, *Care Matters: Time for Change* (DfES, 2007a), outlined a range of proposals to improve outcomes for children in care. It is hoped that those entering the care system will achieve the aspirations we have for all children and will reduce the gap in outcomes between children in care and their peers; also, that it will improve placement stability and ensure more consistency for children in care and improve the experience that children in care have at school and increase their educational attainment.

The government paper *Every Parent Matters* (DfES, 2007b) aims to promote both the development of services for parents as well as their involvement in shaping those services for themselves and their children. Two issues are highlighted: parental engagement, and information for parents and carers. Of particular importance is that of engagement between schools and parents, which is to be enhanced with programmes designed to develop children's social and emotional skills to promote positive behaviour, attendance, learning, and well-being.

The extended schools service, which works with local agencies, provides school-based access to a wide range of services such as child care, study support, parenting support, family learning, and community use of facilities. Parent Support Advisors will also enable parent's access information and specialist services.

The school-based location of programmes to support parents and carers can help change the parental perception of school as a more inclusive institution, but it is not clear to what extent school staff are active participants in the range of programmes. If children and young families are going to make the most of the opportunities offered to them both by their carers and by the educational system, this will require careful attention to their psychological needs. We know that change is possible through putting in place good alternative care, but specialist support also needs to be put in place to support these children, their carers, and other professionals who are part of the network. This can be provided by specialist child & adolescent mental health staff who can offer support training and direct work.

Theoretical frameworks

In our experience, a number of concepts from family therapy and attachment theory are useful when thinking about children in the care system. This work requires interdisciplinary and multi-agency collaborations. From a systemic perspective, the idea that "the whole is more than the sum of its parts" (Salmon & Faris, 2006) offers a valuable contribution to the complexities of such collaborations because it considers different perspectives of professional participants, such as the individual and his or her agency within a wider context of community.

Central to systemic theory is that of social interactions, in which meanings between people emerge. There is some unpredictability in the way two people come to have a conversation, how they will talk together, how they will understand each other, and the relationship they may have after the conversation. Systemic theory considers this to be a constantly evolving process between people rather than as determined by the innate characteristics of each person.

It is not uncommon for parents and teachers to come together with widely differing explanations for a young person's behaviour. For example, at a meeting to discuss the behaviour of a 12-year-old boy, described as disruptive in class and non-compliant in school, his teacher put forward the view that the parents needed to set firmer boundaries and support the teaching staff. The parents thought the school were being unfair and were making false assumptions about their son's role in the classroom difficulties. However, in conversation these views may shift and develop or may become more entrenched. Systemic ideas about understanding the wider contexts in which people live—for example, the experience of a looked-after child—can often allow different ways of understanding the situation to emerge. For example, a head teacher considered that a boy was being inappropriately loud in class, but it emerged in a conversation with his parents facilitated by CAMHS professionals that his parents were of the view that a boy of 9 years should speak clearly and loudly when addressed by a teacher. He also had a hearing difficulty, which his adoptive parents were unaware of until recently. This lack of early screening in looked-after children is not uncommon.

We find the idea of discourse helpful here. Discourse refers to a set of meanings, statements, metaphors, images, stories, and representations that produce versions of events in particular ways. The use of language is a key component because various meanings of a discourse are made available through language, either in conversations, literature, the media, newspaper articles, advertising or even in the meanings embodied in physical appearance or the clothes we wear. All convey messages and meanings that can be "read". For example, discourses in education include ideas such as "children should respect teachers", "parents support in children's education is important", and "children have a right to an education". These reflect ideas about how children, parents, and teachers should behave, and such discourses exert a powerful influence on the day-to-day interaction between people within and outside education.

Social constructionism

Social constructionism proposes that beliefs of individuals are not simply created and maintained within families, but that people—that is, the ideas people have about how they relate and behave towards one another—absorb the beliefs of a particular culture within which they exist (Dallos & Draper, 2000). The belief system of a family is formed and maintained by the pattern of behaviours and interactions of family members. Some families use sayings, catchphrases, or mottos to describe their beliefs—for example, that "Education is important to succeed in society". This value can be an organizing principle of parental behaviour for those parents who wish their children to do well at school. However, children who develop different beliefs and meanings about education can experience difficulties if these conflict with parental beliefs about education. Educational professionals also carry personal and professional beliefs about their school, children, and families and how they connect to learning, behaviours, and relationships. Beliefs can range from considering the importance of parental contributions to education, to families as the cause of the child's difficulties at school. These ideas inform and impact upon the kind of interactions that teachers have with each other and with professionals, children, and their families.

Wider discourses of social care—for example, *Every Child Matters* guidance (DfES, 2004), child protection, *Every Parent Matters* (DfES, 2007b)—impact upon how staff are to deliver the curriculum and support for children and their families within wider social frameworks.

Another useful set of systemic ideas that can be used in educational contexts was developed by Cronen and Pearce (1982). Their model of social interaction highlighted the fact that people behave differently according to social contexts and, furthermore, that they have a hierarchical and reciprocal relationship with one another. For example, a child may act and feel like a different person at home, at school, with friends, and so on, and he or she is shaped by these relationships and interactions. When teachers and parents come together to discuss a child, these different sets of relationships and interactions become evident; both teachers and parents may then experience some confusion as they hear stories from each other of a child different from the one they know. The contexts of home and school create different behaviours and relationships for the child.

> For example, Social Care services have agreed to take a 15-year-old boy into care following repeatedly aggressive behaviour by the boy, who physically threatens his mother. His behaviour needs to be considered within the context of the *episode* in which the aggression occurs—for example, what had caused him to become angry, what had occurred before his physical threats? The episode should be viewed within the context of the *mother–son relationship*— for example, how would they describe their relationship, was the boy always aggressive, when he was not showing aggression how did he and his mother get on? Their relationship needs to be understood within the context of *family script*— for example, what are the family's beliefs about aggression and argument, should children not express anger towards a parent, do parents always have to demonstrate that they are in charge of their family? And the family script has to be considered within cultural ideas about *parental rights and their expectations of children*. Each of these contexts influence each other. The removal of the child then impacts upon the relationships between family members, the child's beliefs about himself and being in the care system, and the professional system of social care, residential care services, mental health services, youth offending team, and the school.

The model can be adapted to include other levels to include the professional and personal contexts, as described in detail elsewhere (Lindsey, 1993).

What is particularly helpful here is that the focus on agency ethos also plays an important role in how the therapist's viewpoint or moral order may be part of the agency ethos or may be subjugated by policies and guidelines of the agency ethos. Sociocultural norms are part of the society by which we live and operate professionally.

School culture

Schools have distinctive identities and cultural practices shaped by governmental, legislative, and educational discourses but also by head teachers and their staff. School culture has also been influenced by social changes to include no corporal punishment, diverse cultural and linguistic groups and teachers, as well as alterations to the curriculum. A major change for schools is the link between parental involvement in children's learning and the extent to which parental aspirations and encouragement can contribute to cognitive development, literacy, and numeracy skills.

Another important development in school culture is the link between emotional health, well-being, behaviour, and learning (DfES, 2006b). An emotionally healthy school culture is one where positive core values have been embedded and the self-esteem of pupils and staff have been enhanced. Relationships are characterized by trust and respect, staff and pupils have positive interactions, are physiologically safe, everyone has a sense of belonging, people work in partnerships, and all have the opportunities to grow in confidence and independence. Schools achieve these goals through their relationships with other agencies that provide broad strategies and services and support, of which CAMHS are one of many.

Multi-agency collaboration

Marked differences between the ways in which different professional groups conceptualize their roles, purposes, and practices can influence the extent to which such differences can contribute to, or hinder, collaborative practices. A number of reasons for ineffective collaboration include lack of trust between agencies, professional claims to aspects of case management, lack of resources to support ongoing collaboration, context of the work, previous history

between agencies, communication difficulties arising from differing professional "languages" and different problem perspectives,
and different agendas of agencies.

The importance of developing a common language between
professionals has been highlighted—that is, professionals who
used the same words to each other but with different meanings,
thereby thinking that they were in agreement with each other
but, in fact, were not (Salmon, 2004). One common experience is
the assumption in education that the needs of the child will not
be recognized or met by safeguarding procedures unless a high
threshold has been met. One effect of this can be professionals'
wish to describe a child's behaviour as extremely worrying and of
concern to others. Paradoxically this can have the effect of parents
and other professionals wishing to downplay the seriousness of the
behaviour in question.

Successful collaborations have been found to lie in effective
communication, common goals, the ability to respect and trust
others, and other factors that include having good working relationships with professionals in other agencies. In our experience,
this is an area that a community-based CAMHS professional is
well placed to offer.

Case study

For example, one of us, based in a secondary school, was involved
in negotiating the changes of "in-school" provision for a looked-
after child. The school proposed moving the child from a specialist unit to mainstream provision. In the autumn of 2004, Mehra,
an unaccompanied minor 12 years of age, arrived in Britain from
Eritrea. As with many such children, little is known of Mehra's
background except that she spent her primary years in Eritrea, that
her father is no longer alive, and that her mother is either a political
or religious prisoner. She travelled to Britain with an adult who left
her at the airport upon her arrival in the country. Mehra was placed
in foster care with a carer from Ethiopia who also spoke Mehra's
first language, Tigrinya. Mehra spoke very little English and began
to attend a local secondary school.

Following her arrival at the school, staff found Mehra's behaviour challenging, and, following a fixed-term exclusion, she was

placed on a reduced timetable. A referral was made to the Multi-Agency Liaison Team, a multidisciplinary child & adolescent mental health team who work with families in Social Services.

The reason for the referral was not only because of Mehra's difficulties in school; an episode of Mehra crawling under a table in a classroom and "barking like a dog" caused school staff to be very concerned and anxious about her mental well-being, and so they sought a psychiatric assessment. Staff requested that Mehra attend an in-patient unit.

In response to the school's description of Mehra as "psychotic", the mental health team considered the possibility of other stories and descriptions of Mehra that were possible, and her relationships with students, staff, foster-carer, and the carer's family, and they sought further information from the professional system. They also considered the impact upon Mehra of having to engage with a psychiatric service and whether this would further impede her fragile emotional state. The school and mental health cultures entered into a dialogue about Mehra. School staff tried to make sense of Mehra's behaviour of crawling under the table and barking in terms of this being a "psychotic" episode that represented something outside their experience as teachers. The mental health professionals considered whether this was a one-off episode, part of a pattern of emotions and behaviours that Mehra displayed in response to particular events. The culture of the school was founded on problem solving and "firing", and the culture of the mental health team was to observe Mehra in the school and consider the episode in terms of the school context and her adjustment to British culture and her foster-family. It was within this context that, as a school-based systemic practitioner, the mental health team referred Mehra to me.

The school provided individual support for Mehra in various ways. During this time Mehra also saw the art therapist at the school, and the educational psychologist began an assessment for a statement of special educational needs to support Mehra's challenging behaviours. She also had a mentor from a local voluntary agency whom she spent time with outside school hours but paid for by the school. She also talked with her tutor at the end of the day to discuss any difficulties. Mehra, who found it difficult to socialize with her peers, developed relationships with two female assistants in the school whose job was to monitor the behaviour of children at break times. She spent these informal periods either in the library, talking with the assistants, or seeing the art therapist, school counsellor, school nurse, or myself. In effect, Mehra developed her "family" within the school—those professionals with whom she felt at ease and who were caring and mindful towards her.

Given Mehra's initial reluctance to engage with me because she feared that there was "something wrong" with her, it seemed more appropriate that she should choose when to visit my office before she agreed to meet for a longer period. Although restless, Mehra talked of Eritrea, her foster-family, her lessons, and other children. She clearly enjoyed learning, and one of her frustrations was that of her use and understanding of the English language. Mehra was operating in her second or even third language and was doing well in some subjects. I was reminded of Burck's (2004) work on living in a second language in which she observes that "Research in various fields had discovered significant differences when bilingual/ multilingual individuals used their different languages" (p. 316).

Although the school had acknowledged Mehra's status as an asylum-seeker who had experienced considerable hardship and trauma in coming to England alone at a young age, they seemed to have paid less attention to Mehra's linguistic adjustments and her high levels of frustration. Clearly intelligent, Mehra found herself disempowered in her learning and in her social interactions with her peers.

Rutter's ideas on resilience were also useful in my work with Mehra. Rutter (1999) defined resilience as "a term used to describe relative resistance to psychosocial risk experiences". He notes that individual qualities of the child and positive school experiences are important protective factors in developing resilience. Based in the school, I was able to have regular, informal conversations with Mehra's tutor, her head of year, and the two assistants about their observations and interactions with her. I considered it important that the school's efforts and support for Mehra should be positively connoted while also highlighting Mehra's resilience in being able to study in a robust school environment and to learn in another language. I also noted that her personal qualities, which she had used to create the school-based "family", indicated her individual qualities that were increasingly recognized by the professionals.

Attachment theory

Attachment research consistently shows that early experience impacts on later capacity (Grossman, Grossman, & Waters, 2005) and that secure attachment in early childhood is significantly related to later good functioning, and insecure attachment to later emotional and behavioural difficulties. Securely attached children have greater capacity for symbolic functioning, are more confident, and more goal oriented and persistent, showing more autonomy in learning, better interaction with peers, and social competence. Children who have had inconsistent care often develop defensive reactions, however good the potential in their placement may be. Children who have been traumatized, neglected, and abused can place enormous psychological pressure on their carers and other important adults in their lives such as teachers and teaching staff. They are often inadvertently trying to communicate the emotional impact of their own experiences. They can become identified with abusive birth parents and be verbally or physically abusive to their carers and/or teachers and peers. They may also provoke violent or aggressive feelings in others. They can communicate their emotional experiences in such a way that those responsible for them feel inadequate, hopeless, incompetent, and lacking self-worth. These sorts of behaviours and feelings can be particularly challenging in educational contexts when those responsible for the children have larger groups of other children's needs to consider. Paradoxically, the traditional behavioural approaches or short-term exclusions of children and young people within the school environment can exacerbate the problems that are inhibiting their ability to access achieving and learning.

A good example of what we have been describing is a young boy, Jack, who, with his sister Rebecca was placed for adoption when he was nearly 4 years of age. His sister was just a little over two years his senior. The children had been removed from the care of their parents on grounds of neglect and were then placed in a foster placement; concerns then arose about the quality of the care the children were receiving there. They were then removed following allegations of neglect on the part of the foster-carers and settled well into a second foster placement before moving to their adoptive family. Both children settled in with their adoptive parents well, but Jack had particular difficulties in interacting with peers, particularly in a group setting. He was described as having a short fuse and would periodically hit out at peers. He was also described as demanding and pushing of boundaries and had difficulties in concentrating, although this had improved as he had settled into his family. He also had particular fears around night-time, darkness, and clouds, with aggressive and often destructive play. The school Jack went to was very sensitive to his needs and, following a meeting with the parents and ourselves, delayed his transition into Year 1 by a year as he was unable to cope in a classroom setting. Although this aspect of Jack's behaviour has improved, he continues to have difficulties in interacting with others and has been considered by his class teachers to be quite dangerous at times in the classroom.

In common with many such families, the adoptive parents, who are extremely committed and attuned to their children's needs, were hopeful that if they provided them with the care and nurturing they had missed when small, eventually their difficulties would be resolved and they would leave their past behind. As is often the case, as these children became more settled with their parents and confident of their permanency, so some of their earlier difficulties began to emerge. Jack's sister showed signs that she may have been sexually abused by her mother and had played a central role in protecting her brother. Jack's adoptive parents began to feel increasingly despondent about their children's future despite having positive reports from the school in terms of their academic achievements. Both children were intrinsically very able and were showing an ability to learn. Jack, however, continued to find it almost impossible to interact with his peers, and on one occasion his classroom teacher removed all the children from the classroom and left him on his own because she considered him to be a danger to the others. The effect this had on Jack was, unsurprisingly, for him to feel increasingly isolated, dangerous, and worthless. His adoptive mother in turn also felt attacked, bitter, and angry, and we were able to use these feelings to help her think not only of some of Jack's experiences but also to frame this as a result of the love she had for her children and the attachment that had clearly taken place.

It is now six years on, and Jack's parents and his school are facing secondary transfer. It is often hard for the parents and the school to see the progress that Jack has made. He has been invited to birthday parties, can now play in the playground, and is making good academic progress. However, this has been a very troubled passage. On many occasions, the anger the school has felt towards Jack due to his aggressive behaviour towards other children, coupled with the school's own sense of worthlessness and inability to control him, has almost resulted in his total exclusion from school. Although Jack has weekly individual psychotherapy, which he has benefited from enormously, a major part of work for his individual psychotherapist and myself has been working with the network and enabling the parents and teachers to develop a shared view of the meaning of Jack's behaviour. Neither fully grasped the impact of Jack's early experiences on his inabilities to concentrate, remember instructions, and control his impulses. Each often felt very critical of the other. When school and parents were divided, Jack's behaviour was at its worst. When they shared a view and supported one another, things were easier. This entailed regular multi-agency meetings at Jack's school, to which everyone was committed.

Implications for practice

There are a number of important themes for professional practice in working with looked-after children and young people in relation to education. The increased awareness of professionals, foster-carers, kinship carers, and adoptive parents of the experiences of looked-after children (reasons for being in care, relationships within and separation from their families of origin, multiple carers, changing schools, peer relationships), and how these experiences impact upon behaviours that are challenging, can support their learning and social relationships.

Attachment theory offers a significant contribution to educationalists and clinicians who work with looked-after children and young people. Secure attachment in early life is related to later good functioning, whereas less secure attachment is related to later emotional and behavioural difficulties that can be particularly challenging in educational contexts. However, schools can provide a secure, consistent base with structure and routine in which looked-after children can function.

Looked-after children often experience many changes not only in terms of the carers but also of the professionals in their lives. The professional network, as a system, plays an important role in the lives of these children and young people. Although individual professionals may change, the network can represent a consistent group who meet regularly and may be experienced by the child as holding an ongoing narrative of his or her life—that is, "holding them in mind". Systemic thinking enables practitioners from a range of professional backgrounds and organizations, with their differing priorities and working practices, to explore their differences and any inherent contradictions that may block multi-agency working, in order to develop a coherent network.

Similarly, educationalists can find systemic thinking and ways of understanding the positions of others—such as those of the young person and of their carers, parents, teaching and support staff—useful in enabling them to consider new ways of working and alternative strategies that may contribute to improved home/school relationships.

Systemic thinking acknowledges the evolving nature of relationships and can help children and their carers and parents to harness the positive aspects of change in the lives of looked-after children and young people. Engagement with ideas of change encourages people to think about its possibilities and how this can build on their personal strengths and resilience. Focusing on the positive aspects of how people work together is an integral part of systemic thinking, and it contributes to maintaining a hopeful and positive relationship between those working with groups experiencing particular difficulties.

Conclusions

As systemic practitioners, we are aware that family life is varied and can be challenging. For those caring for looked-after and adopted children and young people, there may be additional layers of complexity. These include the experience of the children and young people themselves, the families' experiences and expectations, as well as those of the education and social care systems. We believe systemic thinking can be helpful in enabling those caring for children and young people to understand the different meanings of what can be challenging behaviours. We have found that focusing on communication and intervention can help those involved to develop more shared understanding and ways of working with these children and young people. Being able to value the many perspectives within the family and networking contributes to this process. When CAMHS professionals are able to develop good working relationships within schools, this helps to develop a successful partnership.

CHAPTER ELEVEN

Families and schools—a network of interdependent agencies: the ecology of development

Laura Fruggeri

Research in developmental psychology documents how children grow in complex environments (Bronfenbrenner, 1979), how they are able to deal with complex social situations since the early stages (Stern, 1985), and how actively they participate in triangular relationships (Fivaz-Depeursinge & Corboz-Warnery, 1999). Thanks to the studies conducted from both a systemic and an ecological perspective, we have many descriptions of the relational interdependent world of children; of how their growth is connected to the quality of their relationships with their parents and other significant people; and of how they actively interconnect with the different persons that are parts of their lives.

Such an interconnected context of child development underlines the fact that families do not grow children in a vacuum—they do it as part of a larger social and interpersonal network composed of interconnected families, schools, groups, relatives, teachers, peers, friends, professionals, and so on. It is through the participation in this system of interactions that children develop a sense of self, an identity. It is through the participation in this complex relational and institutional network that they construct ties and develop ways of making sense of the world around them. If we take the school, for example, we can say that while learning how to read and write, children also confirm or change the sense of self, make up an image of how the world is, and confirm or change the degree of importance that relationships with others have in their lives.

Even if mainstream developmental psychology still has the dyadic relationship as the fundamental point of reference—that is, the mother–child relationship, the father–child relationship, the parent's relationship, the teacher–pupil relationship, the teacher–family relationship, and so on—the observation of the world of children from an ecological and systemic point of view shows that the minimum size of relational interpersonal and social contexts is never dyadic, but always triadic (Fruggeri, 2002a).

No matter what they do, or with which situation they deal, children, as everybody else, are always involved in relationships of relationships. According to Bronfenbrenner (1979), one relational context is a positive developmental context for a child as long as the relationship with other relational contexts is also positive, and as far as what happens in a relational context has positive repercussions in any other one that is significant for the child. In other words, the context within which children grow is characterized by a *relational interdependence* (Fruggeri, 2005a).

The notion of relational interdependence

From recent research in social psychology, in developmental psychology, and in communication theory, we can point out two considerations that will be useful for the definition of *relational interdependence*. The two considerations are the following:

‣ While interacting, people do not only influence reciprocal experiences, goals, preferences, opinions, or behaviours; they also influence the definition of self, of their relationships, of the episodes they are involved in, and of the broader context of which they are part and within which they construct their ties and relationships.

⋗ In triadic contexts—as all contexts of interactions are—the interdependence is relational: the relationship between two partners
has an effect on the relationships that each one of them has with
others.

These two considerations lead to important theoretical consequences. Because of their triadic and interconnected form, the
interpersonal contexts are characterized by *relational interdependence*—that is, the meaning of the relationship between two people
is dependent not only on the negotiation between the partners
directly involved, but also on the quality of the relationship they
have with others, and on the negotiation taking place between
them. Conversely, the meanings that two partners negotiate
through their direct interactions will have some sort of repercussion on relationships with others who are directly or indirectly
involved.

It may be useful to underline that the notion of *relational interdependence* is different from that of *circularity*, formulated within
first-order cybernetics. In fact, the notion of circularity describes
how behaviours of interacting people affect one another. So, for
example, we can say that the way a teacher acts with a pupil will
affect the way the pupil will act towards his or her parents, which
in turn will affect the way they act towards their child's teacher.
Instead, the notion of relational interdependence describes how
the relationship that two people develop through their interactions affects the relationship that each one of them constructs with
others to whom they are connected. So, for example, we can say
that the relationship developed between a teacher and a child will
affect, somehow, the relationship that the child has with his or her
parents, which in turn will affect the relationship that parents and
teacher will develop, which will feed back and affect the relationship that teacher and child will maintain or change. In other words,
the notion of circularity refers to reciprocal influence of *behaviours
and actions*, whereas the notion of relational interdependence refers
to the reciprocal influence of *relationships*.

If we move from the perspective of children and take the point
of view of the professionals working with children in the social-
psychological and educational field, the above considerations allow

us both to draw on the interconnected interpersonal and institutional network within which school professionals operate and to suggest interesting reflections.

The interconnected context of professional interventions

Once we place the professionals at the centre of the scene, we can describe them almost with the same words that we used in describing the world of children and their families.

In fact, we may underline that professionals do not help (teach, support, cure, monitor, consult with) children in a vacuum; they do it as part of a larger social and interpersonal network. They are involved in complex relationships even when they are not aware of it, or even when they work in isolation in their private offices. Professionals work in networks comprising, for example, interconnected families, schools, groups, parents, teachers, colleagues, teams—networks within which people construct identities, relationships, and social worlds. In other words, while professionals teach, cure, help, support, control, consult, they also participate in a context of interactions within which the people involved develop, maintain, or change a sense of self, of others, of the situations they deal with, and of the world in which they live.

In the face of such interconnected contexts, the question that I want to raise is the following: "To what extent are professionals aware of the complexity of the context in which they operate?" Such a question is relevant from a methodological point of view because professionals plan their interventions not only according to their theoretical models, but also according to the idea they have of the relational context of which they are a part, and according to the idea they hold of the effect that their actions may have on others.

The above question can be further articulated in more specific questions:

▹   "What are the representations that school professionals hold of their relationship with the children's families and other institutional contexts that are significant to them?"

> "What are their representations of the professional system they are part of in relation to children and their families and other interpersonal and institutional contexts?"

> "What effects do they think their interventions have on children and their families?"

A study conducted with different types of professionals working in the educational system (teachers, social workers, psychologist, paediatricians, child psychiatrists) has pointed out several different representations that can be helpful in trying to answer the above questions (Ingrosso, 1997).

The representations of the context
of professional interventions

As to the representations that school professionals have of their relationship with the children's families and significant systems, we found five different models (Fruggeri, 1998).

1. *The model of the "isolated child".* The relationship that the child has with his or her family or other relational context is ignored or considered irrelevant for the intervention carried out by the professionals in a school context. Starting from this premise, questions about the relational world of the child are never raised. Professionals are not interested in knowing how the child–family relationship is involved in the presented issue. They do not reflect on the repercussions that their intervention can have on the child–family relationship or on other significant implied relationships. They never wonder how such repercussions can reverberate in the realization of their intervention.

2. *The model of "parallel convergence".* This model can be described as following: professionals working in school contexts conceive of themselves and the child's family as separate entities, each one of which has important and significant relationships with the child, even if in separate and unrelated fields. As above, also from this point of view, the interdependent system of

school professionals', children's, and families' relationships and actions is not considered.

3. *The model of unilateral collaboration.* Starting from the considera- tion that families are important relational contexts for children's growth, families are involved in the process of intervention as a "means" for rendering the intervention of the school profes- sionals more effective. Families are considered a resource for the professionals, who nevertheless do not consider themselves a resource for the family but only for the child, who remains the target of the intervention. In this model, the connection among the different interpersonal contexts implied in the process of intervention is considered, but it is a linear connection and not a relational interdependent connection: the family's behaviours and relationships are thought of as being influential on the professional intervention, but not vice versa. In other words, from this point of view, professionals reflect on the influence that family–child relationship could have on the outcome of the intervention, but they do not reflect on the repercussion that their intervention can have on the child–family relationship, and they never consider how such repercussions can reverber- ate in the realization of the intervention itself.

4. *The model of substitution.* This is the opposite of the previ- ous model: the family is considered to be the cause of all the child's problems. Starting from this premise, the child–family relationship is evaluated as a negative element in the child's life. Consequently, it is judged as an element that has to be eliminated and substituted by a relationship between the child and the professional system. The relationship of child with pro- fessionals is emphasized and reinforced to the detriment of the relationship with his or her family, without any reflection upon the consequence that such a fracture can have on the child's development.

5. *The co-evolutionary interdependent model.* From this perspec- tive, all events occurring within the context of the relationship between a professional and a child trigger processes within the context of the relationship between the latter and his or her significant system; these processes, in turn, influence the evolution and outcome of the intervention that is carried on

within the context of interactions between professional and child. This model guides a professional to wonder about the meaning that the intervention planned for a child could have within the context of the relationship between the child and his or her family. Such questioning would lead the professional to plan an intervention not simply following the criterion of what can be useful and helpful for the child, but according to in what way it can be useful and helpful for the child as a component of a family system.

* * *

As to the representations of the school professional system in relation to children and their families, we have two different perspectives: the *we/them perspective* versus the *interdependent system perspective*.

The *we/them perspective* looks at the situation of intervention only from the point of view of professionals, who conceive of the relationship between professional and child as a face-to-face interaction with no connection with the broader context within which the interaction takes place. The main characters (professionals and children) are described in an abstract way insofar as their belonging and significant relationships are not considered as relevant to the understanding of the situation and to the planning of the intervention.

From the *interdependent system perspective*, instead of the professional system, the child and his or her family are seen as an interdependent network of many different, interrelated, and interconnected characters (professionals, clients, and their significant systems). The professionals are aware of being part of such a complex network and, in order to make sense of the situation and to plan the proper intervention, consider the belonging and relationships of all the characters involved to be important elements.

As to the representations of the effects of interventions carried out by professionals, we have two different approaches: the *instructive approach* versus the *constructionist approach*.

The *instructive approach* is based on a linear causal model. It describes the interventions of professionals as actions that can modify or have an effect on children *per se*. The intervention is an application of technique, methodologies, theories, and procedures.

The professional is an expert implementing his or her knowledge in order to influence the child's life. From this point of view, professionals behave as if only their single actions had an effect on the situation, as if the relationship that is generated from the interaction with the child would not have any repercussion on the outcome of their interventions.

The *constructionist approach*, instead, emphasizes the process of communication embedded in any intervention, a process through which identities, relationships, social worlds are constructed. From this point of view, the relationship that is generated from the inter-action with the child during the realization of the intervention is considered an element that has important repercussions on the outcome of the intervention. Moreover, the relationship develop-ing among the professional, the child, and his or her significant system—that is, family, but not only that—is considered an ele-ment contributing to the construction of the intervention.

The idea of the relational context and the idea of the effects of professionals' actions can be independent one from another. For example, a professional can be systemic and instructive. It is the case of a professional who emphasizes and evaluates the relationships involved in the situation of the intervention without, though, considering the effect that the relationships contingently developed can have on the outcome of the intervention. More and more professionals working in the educational field take into consideration the network of relationships in which children are involved, but this does not necessarily mean that they also evaluate the possible effects that their specific relationship with them could have on the process of intervention. In other words, relationships can be considered only as a channel for understanding and not as a dynamic element contributing to construct the intervention.

The two levels of an intervention

The ideas of interdependence and social construction suggest the adoption of two levels of analysis for the understanding of the processes implied in any intervention (Fruggeri, 1998, 2002b):

the level of the *individual construction* and the level of *co-construction*.

When we choose to describe *the level of individual construction* involved in an interaction, we focus on how people take part in interactive processes. From this perspective, it is possible to point out the ways in which people make sense of their world(s), including themselves, others, and the situations they cope with, and how they act accordingly. When we describe the individual level of construction, we underline how people take part in interactions, so we stress feelings, meanings, goals, and behaviours. We may also indicate how behaviours are connected to feelings that are connected to meanings, which in turn are connected to behaviours that are connected to goals. However, while the participants in the interaction are engaged in these complex symbolic, behavioural, strategic processes, they also initiate a "dance" through which they negotiate and co-construct meanings, identities, relationships, roles, and social realities. When we choose to describe this joint process, we point out the *level of co-construction*. From this perspective, we do not emphasize how people take part in an interaction; rather, we focus on what they do together.

The distinction between the individual and the co-construction levels of interaction is helpful when distinguishing between different levels of analysis of any process of intervention (Fruggeri, 1998, 2002b). At one level (individual construction), we focus on the professional—on his or her thoughts, intentions, decisions, and language. We could of course have talked of goals, descriptions, ideas, and theoretical models, or even of prejudices, values, ideology, and actions. At the individual construction level of analysis, we pay attention to how all these elements connect with each other in a pattern that could be defined as "the way the professional participates in the interaction with the client". The individual construction level of analysis points out the reflexivity between theoretical framework, attribution of meaning (descriptions), and actions. In fact, it is according to a theoretical model that professionals describe the situation as they do, and it is according to what they describe and to their theoretical model (or to their philosophical stance) that they make decisions to do this or that in order to help the client.

Professionals are not the only ones who individually construct and act in the situation. Clients are engaged in the same kind of process. Clients do not have formal theoretical models to refer to; they have naive or implicit theories according to which they also make sense of what is happening and then act. They respond to professionals' interventions according to the sense they make of what the professionals do—that is, according to their own way of constructing the situation and in order to achieve their own goals, whatever these may be.

While professional and client are engaged in their individual processes of construction, they also participate together in a cooperative dance, a joint action through which they negotiate and co-construct who they are, what they are doing together, and what the situation is that they are involved in. The analysis of this level of the process of intervention does not pertain to the professionals' ideas or actions, goals, or expectations, nor to the clients' ideas, actions, goals, or expectations. At this level, the analysis implies a description of interactions—that is, of the joint action of therapist and client and of the meanings generated through it.

Let us describe the relational context of an intervention in a client's words—no technical or scientific language could do it better:

> I would not always overcome my exasperation. But even then I was frequently influenced by a spirit of bravado and defiance of the doctors, to whom I knew my letters were subjected for inspection; I was determined, if they declared that my anger at being confined, and at my treatment, was a proof of my madness, that they should have evidence enough of it. . . . Even a deeper motive lay hid under all this violence of expression; and this may perhaps by many be deemed an insane motive: I knew that, of all the torments to which the mind is subject, there is none so shocking, so horrid to be endured as that of remorse for having injured or neglected those who deserved our esteem and consideration. I felt for my sisters, my brothers, and my mother: I knew they could not endure to look upon what they had done towards me, to whom they were once so attached, if they rightly understood it; that they could know no relief from the agony of that repentance which comes too late, gnawing the very vitals, but in believing me partly unworthy of their

affection; and therefore I often gave the reins to my pen, that they might hereafter be able to justify themselves, saying he has forfeited our respect—he has deserved our contempt, and merited our abandonment of him. [John Perceval's *Narrative of the Treatment Experienced by a Gentleman*, 1840, reported in Bateson, 1978, p. 49]

When professionals talk about the processes of their interventions, they often confine their conversations to a narrow context, that of the professional–client interaction (the client being a person or a family). All that is outside it seems to disappear, as if clients changed or stayed the same only because of what happens in the context of their relationship with professionals. However, as John Perceval explains to us, the way clients respond to professionals is connected with the meaning that whatever happens in the setting of the intervention has with respect to other contexts of relationship, and whatever is going on in these relationships affects the process of intervention. The interpersonal process taking place during the realization of an intervention is then part of a broader network of interdependent relationships.

The "double description"

Most of the time, school professionals take the perspective of the individual construction level in order to make decisions as to what sense they can make of the situation and as to what is the most proper thing to do in the situation. Most of the time, the perspective of the individual level is enough to guide the professionals to plan interventions that turn out to be helpful for the children and their families. Taking a different perspective from that of the co-construction level for planning the intervention does not, however, mean that the relational processes are not active in the realization of the intervention. It is only a choice of level of analysis. Yet sometimes it can be necessary to analyse the situation from the relational/constructive level. It could be that what happens in the context of the intervention makes sense only if we consider the relational processes implied. Those are the cases when a double description (Bateson, 1979) becomes useful—that is, a description of the situation from both the individual and the relational/constructive level (Fruggeri, 1998). The two levels of analysis described above do not exclude each other; rather, they complement each other, since they clarify different types of elements co-occurring and co-contributing to the construction of the outcome of the intervention.

From the individual level, we can analyse the child relational dynamics, interactions, needs, behaviours, feelings, resources, aims, desires—and anything else relevant in his or her life—in order to individuate the most proper intervention.

Taking the perspective of the relational/constructive level, we are invited to reflect on professional premises and actions and on how they contribute to construct the relationship with others. But, overall, we are invited to reflect on the meaning that one's own intervention has within the child's relational context. The method of the double description opens new perspectives. Considering the individual and the relational levels implied in an intervention, we might be able to see that risks and resilience are not only in children or in their families. We might be able to see that they are embedded in relationships.

Different levels of professional competence and responsibility

The two levels of analysis described above imply two different levels of professional competence.

The individual/strategic level of analysis requires a competence that we could define as *technical*—that is, a competence that relies on the knowledge of techniques, theories, and methodologies and on the ability to apply them and use them in connection with the specific people, situations, events, contexts that professionals have to deal with.

The relational/constructive level of analysis, instead, requires a different type of competence: a competence of a second order that we could define as *relational*—that is. the capacity to reflect on the meaning that the exercise of the technical competence has within the relationship with the client and his or her significant system.

The practice of relational competence contributes to the construction of interactive contexts within which clients develop the answers to their needs. The practice of relational competence is not a statement about the ability of the professional; rather, it contributes to the construction of an interactive situation within which clients can develop their own competence. The relational competence does not intervene upon someone but with someone. The different levels of competence described above imply also two different levels of responsibility: technical and relational.

While the technical responsibility binds professionals to a correct application of a model of intervention, the relational responsibility binds them to have a constant understanding of the interactive process they are engaged in with their clients. Because of their relational responsibility, professionals know that the criterion for deciding whether an idea has worth, whether a notion should be left or taken, whether a belief should be challenged, is not outside the relationship with clients.

Concluding remarks

The individual and relational levels of analysis of the process of intervention, the technical and relational competences, and the technical and relational responsibilities do not exclude each other; rather, they constitute different points of view on professional practice, and the method of double description includes all of them.

CHAPTER TWELVE

The social construction of school exclusion

Sadegh Nashat & Sue Rendall

Children grow up within a network of complex systems. These include the child's own inner world, a system comprising, for example, personality, attribution, innate abilities; the family, a system comprising, for example, culture, dynamics between family members, family structures, family scripts; and the school, system comprising, for example, culture and ethos (Rendall & Stuart, 2005).

This chapter offers an understanding of school exclusion within different levels of contexts and explores how these are interconnected. Historically and geographically, the act of excluding children and young people from school has taken different shapes and significance, largely influenced by social and political processes. Despite claims that policies and educational decision-making are evidence-based, our experience is that there is a resistance to acknowledging different forces that influence those processes, and therefore, perhaps, a denial of the complexities involved.

In the first part of the chapter, we present the theoretical lenses through which we explored the social construction of school exclusion. Later we draw upon case studies to illustrate connections between individual and social narratives. The experiences of being excluded from school, as reported by pupils, parents, and families, professionals and institutions, will be seen through different lenses and, as shown in the subsequent examples, result in different constructions of events—different "truths".

Theoretical lenses

One way of managing complexity is to reduce it by examining parts of the system. This reductionist model will work perfectly well for non-human systems—for example, if the light bulb in a sealed unit of a modern car is faulty, the unit can be replaced with no effect upon the other functioning systems of the car. Tempting as it might be in its apparent simplicity, this will not be effective in addressing the complexities of human relationships, where tinkering with any one aspect of a system of interconnected relationships will inevitably impact upon, and change, the whole system. A more appropriate and meaningful approach is to find ways of understanding the complexities rather than reducing them (Rendall & Stuart, 2005).

One way of addressing complexity in relation to exclusion from school is to adopt a social constructionism approach, by which we will examine and deconstruct school exclusion and present the different meanings attributed to it within a European perspective. We believe that the content of narratives derives from and represents the social and cultural contexts in which events have been experienced, and we include in this narratives of children, parents, and head teachers who have been involved in exclusion from schools.

Social constructionism takes a questioning view of beliefs by assuming that an objective "truth" does not exist. This is not to say that reality does not exist, but, rather, that it is socially constructed (Gergen, 1999). Social constructions are bound within a historical, societal, and cultural framework, and attempts to observe phenomena independently of this context are regarded as highly problematic. It is therefore important to pay attention to how context is influencing and shaping professional practices in relation to school exclusion. Social constructionism has given a central role to language and discursive practices. Language makes use of "discourse" that serves the purpose of constructing objects and, as such, is an active process (Burr, 1995). Gergen's work (1999), in particular, demonstrates that the meaning we assign to the world is generated through language. Gergen is largely influenced by Wittgenstein's (1922) philosophical work on language, which postulates that words have a meaning within a context; the meaning of a word is its use in language. Thus, Gergen (1999) argues that it is through language that we describe the world. Social constructionism does not reject the idea of "truth" but postulates that since we use language, we may socially construct reality as a result of our use of different "languages" (scientific, political, religious, etc.) to describe the same phenomenon.

This means that our vision of reality, the way we assign meaning, or the way we attribute cause to behaviour may also be socially constructed through the language we use. The political, professional, social, and cultural views we hold may influence our description of reality and affect the way we think (Gergen, 1999). An example from Rendall and Stuart (2005) is that of a teacher who asked a disruptive a boy in his lesson, "What's your game, boy?" The boy understood the teacher to be asking him if he was playing with a Game Boy (a portable computer device). The boy denied having a Game Boy, and the teacher perceived this response to be defiant and oppositional rather than a different use of the words "game boy". The consequence, as a direct result of this misunderstanding of language, was that the boy was excluded from the lesson, still not understanding what it was that he had done wrong, and the teacher still believing that the boy had been defiant and oppositional.

This example illustrates how even in the smallest and shortest of exchanges, miscommunication can arise from the different perspectives and experiences of the language being used. Had the teacher been familiar with the adolescent's world of computer games, he might have been able to understand a different meaning and been able to take up a different position.

The importance of language to the way events and experience are perceived has been developed by authors such as Shotter (2000). He argues that the way we see the world is rooted in the way we speak about it:

Our basic person–world relations is both "produced by" and "contained" in our self-conscious experience. Clearly, it is "as if" they were "given" to us by an external agency. We have no awareness of our own involvement in their construction. It is as if our person–world relations are independent of our self–other relationships. [Shotter, 2000, p. 35]

Rendall and Stuart's (2005) study illustrates Shotter's point: both pupils and teachers have very little awareness of how their view of the situation (e.g., the child's behaviour) is constructed by the discourse surrounding them at a school, community, or societal level.

Another aspect of complexity is concerned with the notion of contexts and systems, explored by authors such as Carter and McGoldrick (1989) who describe a model of "layered" systems of influences on the developmental life of the family. The nuclear family, the extended family, and the social systems are in interaction and will influence family patterns and family, community, and social myths and beliefs.

For the purpose of this chapter, we are working within narrative approaches (Payne, 2000), and the theory of coordinated management of meaning (CMM), developed from social psychology (Pearce & Cronen, 1980). CMM postulates that we socially construct meanings in our conversations with each other. It is a way of conceptualizing a hierarchical organization of meanings such that the more abstract contextualizes and defines the less abstract. This approach has had a major influence on systemic thinking and on family therapy, leading to the development of specific psychological interventions and consultation models. By postulating that people co-construct their social realities, a framework that attends to the general (the higher levels) and to the specific (relational or individual levels) contexts of meaning and human behaviour provides a template for analysing the interactions between frames of reference or contexts which has six embedded levels of context in relation to the analysis of families.

Although the number and nature of the levels of contexts is not fixed, Pearce and Cronen (1980) have chosen to identify six levels, and there is an implicit hierarchy whereby the higher levels will influence the lower ones. Each event observed by an individual is part of different levels of meanings that not only are embedded and influenced by the exchanges a family could have with a professional, but are also organized by higher contextual levels that potentially impact upon the thinking of a group of mental health and education professionals discussing the problem of a family.

CMM is concerned with the complexity between the micro-social processes and the cultural totality and aspects in which the micro-social daily life events and processes take place. It is concerned with how we can coordinate and establish meaning, and identity, with each other.

These ideas are closely linked to Bateson's (1979) concept of context. The concept of context is a psychological, philosophical, and epistemological concept, and therefore it is never fixed. Bateson is well known for starting any answer to a question he was given with the words, "This reminds me of a story".

Relational aspects of meaning and beliefs constitute one important level of context. Social constructionism focuses on relationships as a unit, which influences meaning and beliefs in individuals. Over the past four hundred years, there has been a preoccupation for seeing ourselves as individuals, with our own feelings, thoughts, and well-being, and it seems easy to forget that individuals all belong to others and exist only in relation to others (Potter & Wetherell, 2007). One of the ideas often presented in modern existentialist literature is that we are basically alone. There is paradox here, in that one can only speak about being alone in the context of being with others, in the context of relationships. Bateson (1979) was one of the first social scientists to focus on relationships and differences. One can only talk about a relationship if there are at least two different entities. The relationship is something between at least two individuals, groups, other entities. The relationship is nothing in itself. It is something that exists between us, something that connects us and separates us at the same time. Relationships are named, and through this naming process they acquire their significance and identity for those involved.

It is essential when thinking about school exclusion to adopt a narrative approach that assumes that the self is created in stories and that these stories are guidelines (scripts) for actions (White & Epston, 1990). The self can best be explored, experienced and developed, changed or transported by individuals themselves through different practices of telling and re-telling their own stories. The self is constituted through words and meanings that are inherent in the culture. Every experience can only be expressed in words that our culture allows us to use. The self is, therefore, always emerging through the processes of conversation, storytelling, and making meaning from actions that we and others perform and from stories we hear or tell ourselves.

Language serves as a vehicle for the powerful influences of the culture and social belief systems of individuals. We are expected to act within a cluster of rights and responsibilities deriving from our position within the social structure, the community in which we live, and the pattern of conversations in which we are able or required to participate (Harré, 1987). The social process of conferring an identity is so powerful that it is usually invisible. Our selves are part of the process by which we make our social worlds. Patterns of conversations with our parents, brothers and sisters, teachers and pupils, and government officials produce the "self" that we know ourselves to be (Pearce, 2007). The narrative or story metaphor is essentially one of language, both oral and written. However, non-language aspects of experience are incorporated within the concept of narrative, particularly feeling and intentions (Rendall & Stuart, 2005). Some narratives are more dominant than others, and when the dominant narratives are problem-saturated, they may eclipse more enabling narratives (White & Epston, 1990). In the case of pupils being excluded from schools, the dominant narrative is often about a series of individual misdemeanours (i.e., the breaking of school rules) rather than an alternative narrative of a child in need. The question therefore arises: whence does the dominant narrative come?

One of the sources of complexity in human systems is the fact that human interactions are driven by communication (Bateson, 1979), which is usually multifaceted and takes place at a number of verbal and nonverbal levels. Patterns of interaction and communication tend to recur over time and may also be sustained through feedback. A child who gains adult attention through misbehaviour is often using the misbehaviour as a way of getting attention, although not necessarily in a conscious way. Through a different feedback (such as ignoring the misbehaviour and giving attention to appropriate behaviour), the attention-seeking child is likely to employ different (more acceptable) behaviours to gain attention.

These interacting patterns tend to be circular rather than linear, and they give rise to circular, rather than linear, explanations. Circular explanations emphasize the fact that causes reside in the interactional processes between two or more people, rather than solely in individuals.

The adoption of a circular rather than a linear approach to causality takes account of the interrelationships between an individual's systems and moves away from a blame culture, although Dowling and Osborne (1994) emphasizes that since the 1960s clinicians have moved towards placing individuals within the context of their families and systemic family therapy has developed as an alternative to treatment of individual pathology. Similarly, to some extent, educationalists have moved away from solely considering within-child causes to considering how pupils are affected by, for example, particular educational settings to which they belong. However, as Dowling goes on to say, the application of thinking systemically about schools has developed slowly and, in the main, separately from systemic work with families. It is our belief that this is far from a general shift in child & adolescent mental health professionals across Europe. This is unfortunate, as the two kinds of system do share common components and concepts. These include rules, punctuation, culture and belief systems, roles, and authority and power (Dowling & Osborne, 1994).

Linking theory to practice

In a study on professional responses to children with emotional and behavioural difficulties, Nashat (2008) showed that child mental health and education professionals had different ways to attribute cause to children's behaviour. This seemed to be strongly linked to the beliefs and perceptions that each professional group had acquired through their respective training and context of work.

Rendall and Stuart (2005) found that the narrative of many teachers, when describing excluded pupils, reported that they believed that the pupils had orchestrated their exclusion from school. However, excluded pupils themselves reported that the exclusion had come as a great surprise, and, had it been their

intention to avoid being in school, they would have simply tru-
anted rather than behaved in the ways unacceptable to the school.
In the case of the twenty excluded pupils in the Rendall and Stuart
study, all had been excellent school-attenders, and all expressed the
wish to return to full-time education. This example shows that both
pupils and education professionals are in different realities, which
in turn shapes their understanding of the situation.

Neuberger (2005), a French systemic psychotherapist, shows
how families develop myths that will shape their members' behaviour in certain types of interaction and situation. He argues that
families will transmit, from one generation to another, myths that
include experiences and beliefs about school and education.

This idea is close to what Byng-Hall (2008) identifies as family
scripts, which refer to the ways families expect relationships to be
between family members and are transmitted from one generation to the other. Byng-Hall advocates the inclusion of attachment
theory in systemic approaches and shows how an individual's
script for attachment can be linked to behaviour in families. In a
major study on school exclusion, Rendall and Stuart (2005) demonstrate how a parent's own experience of education shapes their
interactions with their child's school. They considered this in relation to protective factors to risk, where mothers' own experience of
school had a significant impact upon their own child's experience
of school. For example, they refer to one mother who described
herself as being "hopeless" at school work, but who had really
enjoyed going to school and had wept when she had to leave at
the age of 15. This mother reported that her own positive experience of school had helped her both to support her own child when
he experienced some difficulties and to be confident to approach
teachers without feeling judged by them. Another mother, who
had been a high achiever at school, reported that she had been
very unhappy there and described her difficulties in being able
to support and encourage her own son; as a consequence, she did
not engage in working with her son's teachers to help him, and
he developed negative attitudes towards his school and teachers
(Rendall & Stuart, 2005).

The concept of family myths and family scripts is equally applicable to higher levels of context. We believe that schools, communities, and societies are influenced by implicit scripts that influence

and shape their beliefs about issues such as social inclusion and exclusion. These myths are subtle and are embedded in the texture of individuals' and societal interactions. Scripts, which generally are conveyed through discourses, can influence future behaviours of families, communities, and social exchanges. However, scripts can be rewritten, and, where this is possible, individuals can be freed from the myths and scripts that have influenced them (Byng-Hall, 1998).

Likewise, we can acknowledge the existence of school scripts, perhaps most easily recognized by considering school ethos. Rendall and Stuart (2005) considered school exclusion experiences in the light of two distinct types of school ethos, as first described by Reynolds and Sullivan (1979). At one extreme is the *coercive school*, in which staff hold negative attitudes towards their pupils, seeing them as being in need of containment, control, and character training. They employ deficiency explanations for the high levels of learning and behaviour difficulties that they observe in their pupils. Teaching and management strategies that are associated with this view tend to be towards the punitive and confrontational: staff–pupil relationships are, by and large, of an impersonal nature.

At the other extreme is the *incorporate school* ethos, where staff hold positive views of pupils and their parents and recognize the essential worth and individuality of each child, and they demonstrate a commitment to the aim of eliciting the voluntary involvement of the pupils and parents in school life. Teaching and management strategies associated with these schools stress pupil responsibility and self-discipline, coupled with pupil involvement in lessons and in the wider life of the school. Staff–pupil relationships tend to be marked by interpersonal rather than impersonal styles, with the stress being put on mutual respect and partnership. Learning and behaviour problems tend to be approached in a therapeutic manner, with the emphasis on the pupils' need for support.

Children and young people can find themselves stuck in the middle of inconsistencies between school scripts and family scripts. Many of these children are able to accommodate such inconsistencies, but vulnerable children are not. Where the inconsistencies are extreme, even the more resilient children can find themselves in conflict with either the family script or the school script. Rendall and Stuart hypothesize that staff in coercive schools perceive the behaviour and attainments of their pupils as justification for their negative attitudes, and that disruptive pupils in such schools often feel that their negative behaviour is a justifiable response to coercive treatment. In incorporative schools, a similarly self-fulfilling but opposite script may be at work. Pupils are subject to the influences of the dominant discourse of the school (as, presumably, are the teachers), adopting modes of adaptation to the institution that serve to perpetuate the prevailing discourse (script), whether or not this is beneficial to all, or any, of the participants in the school organization.

European paradigms

A fundamental difference between the UK way of managing disruptive pupils and the French way is that in the United Kingdom there is a law that permits such action, whereas in France, and in the majority of other EU countries, no such law exists. Zay (2005), in her study, shows that, although there is no official procedure in France to exclude pupils, where schools make it clear to such pupils that their behaviour is not wanted, disruptive pupils choose to exclude themselves. The narrative of these pupils is that they have been left feeling unwanted by the school. Zay (2005) also reports that in these circumstances, both in the United Kingdom and in France, the blame for the exclusion is located solely in the pupil.

When we compare the French system, where there is no law to provide exclusion, with the UK system, where such a law exists and is well used, results for young people are the same—they become socially excluded. To help us to understand this, we need to explore different European perspectives on social inclusion and exclusion which impact upon sociopolitical forces. Cousins (1998) synthesizes different paradigms of social inclusion and exclusion in Europe by studying those paradigms through various lenses, including the concept of citizenship, the debate on the role of the

State, the structure of the labour market, and available social welfare mechanisms. She postulates that more than one paradigm can exist in a country, although there will always be one that is dominant and inspires policy-makers. According to Cousins (1998), two coexisting yet opposing paradigms are found in Europe: the liberal Anglo-Saxon one from the nineteenth century, dominant in the United Kingdom, on the one side, and the Continental "solidarity" paradigm dominant in most European countries, on the other.

The UK paradigm is one where the social excluded (including those excluded from school) are seen as lacking the capacity, the wherewithal, and the motivation to be socially included. The discourse then becomes one of locating blame in the individual, whether the individual is the child, the parent, or the teacher, but not the system or government policies.

The Continental "solidarity" paradigm corresponds to a philosophy of school inclusion where all participants (children, parents, education professionals, and the school) share the view that the school is a space where pupils should be, a place that helps even the less fortunate to acquire the skills to feel included in society. The result is that in countries such as France, Switzerland, or Italy, the exclusion of primary school children is forbidden and is extremely rare in secondary education. This contrasts drastically with the United Kingdom, where, while not actually encouraging exclusion, there is a statutory framework for allowing it. The question already asked in this chapter of "where do the dominant narratives come from?" can be again asked in relation to what might it represent for a country to pass a law that allows for the exclusion of children from school.

Zay (2005) suggests that in the Anglo-Saxon paradigm, the primacy of the neo-liberal approach sees the capacity of young people to learn and be included as an individual responsibility. In the United Kingdom, responsibility for being included lies not with the system (community, school, society) but with the individual.

In a study of cross-cultural comparisons, Zay (2005) presents the argument that social exclusion is linked to poverty. Parsons (1999) supports this view specifically in relation to exclusion from schools, referring to poverty research as being "about what level of income a person needs to function in society, and social exclusion being about the income and resources only insofar as it affects social participation, social integration and access of power" (p. 172).

Conclusions

The United Kingdom has a divisive and competitive school/education system, comprising expensive fee-paying public schools, selective and non-selective State schools and colleges, and faith schools, as well as the opportunity for parents to educate their children at home (or educate otherwise), all within the law requiring compulsory education for children from 5 to 16 years of age. This may give an impression of choice, but for those who do not conform, or are at odds with the requirements of behaviour as dictated by the dominant discourse, the choice is illusory—their choice is one of conform and fit in or else be excluded. Slee (1998) suggests that

> individual student pathology deflects from the harder question about the exclusionary impetus of educational markets as expressed through league tables, test scores and failing schools, which are unable simultaneously to exhibit the preconditions for the effective containment of difficult children and the raising of GCSE scores. [p. 103]

Parsons (1999) refers to UK education policy discourse having moved from that of optimistic and enabling in the 1960s, to that of restrictive and controlling from the 1990s onwards. When schools do not meet government targets—close them. When parents fail to get their children to attend school—fine or even imprison them. When children consistently break the school rules—exclude them. There is a dominant narrative of the "undeserving"—those who, it is assumed, choose not to take advantage of the opportunities provided by government, communities, and schools to decent, law-abiding citizens. The result is that such opportunities are then withdrawn. Is it a coincidence that, despite the enormous increase in expenditure on education in UK schools in the past ten years, over half of the UK prison population (which is the largest in

Europe) has significant difficulties with literacy skills and that the basic skills deficit and the school exclusion experience of the 18- to 20-year-old prison population are a third higher than those of older prisoners?

In this chapter we have tried to demonstrate some of the complexities that exist across European education communities that are involved in addressing the needs of pupils who challenge mainstream education systems. It is clear from the literature and from our own experience that whether or not there is a legal process for excluding pupils from schools, pupils with challenging and disruptive behaviour often find themselves excluded from mainstream education and community settings, in many cases leading them to experience long-term social exclusion. Young people who find themselves in such circumstances report feelings of disempowerment, isolation, and a lack of fundamental education and life skills that might help them to participate in the social, economic, and political life of their community.

REFERENCES

Abraham, K. (1911). *Clinical Papers and Essays on Psychoanalysis*. New York: Brunner/Mazel.

Adamo, S. M. G., Adamo Serpieri, S., Giusti, P., & Tamajo Contarini, R. (2008). Parenting a new institution. In: M. Rustin & J. Bradley (Eds.), *Work Discussion: Learning from Reflective Practice in Work with Children and Families* (pp. 233–254). London: Karnac.

Adamo, S. M. G., & Aiello, A. (2006). Desperately trying to get through: Establishing contact in work with adolescent drop-outs. *International Journal on School Disaffection, 4* (1): 27–38.

Adamo, S. M. G., & Rustin, M. (2001). Editorial. *International Journal of Infant Observation and Its Applications, 4* (2): 3.

Akhtar, S. (1999). *Immigration and Identity: Turmoil, Treatment and Transformation*. Northvale, NJ: Jason Aronson

Atkinson, M., Wilkin, A., Stott, A., Doherty, P., & Kinder, K. (2002). *Multi-Agency Working: A Detailed Study*. Slough: National Foundation for Educational Research.

Ballreich, R., & Glasl, F. (2007). *Mediation in Bewegung. Ein Lehr- und Übungsbuch* [Mediation in motion]. Stuttgart: Concadora.

Bamberger, G. (2001). *Lösungsorientierte Beratung* [Solution-oriented counselling]. Weinheim: Beltz.

Baruch Bush, R. A., & Folger, J. (1994). *The Promise of Mediation: Responding to Conflict through Empowerment and Recognition.* San Francisco, CA: Jossey-Bass.

Bateson, G. (1978). The birth of a matrix or double bind and epistemology. In M. M. Berger (Ed.), *Beyond the Double Bind* (pp. 39–64). New York: Brunner/Mazel.

Bateson, G. (1979). *Mind and Nature.* New York: Dutton.

Beaumont, M. (1991). Reading between the lines: The child's fear of meaning. *Psychoanalytic Psychotherapy, 5* (3): 261–169.

Bick, E. (1964). Notes on infant observation in psychoanalytic training. *International Journal of Psychoanalysis, 45*: 558–566.

Bick, E. (1968). The experience of the skin in early object-relations. *International Journal of Psychoanalysis, 49*: 484–486. Reprinted in M. H. Williams (Ed.), *Collected Papers of Martha Harris and Esther Bick* (pp. 114–118). Strath Tay: Clunie Press, 1987.

Biehal, N., Clayden, J., Stein, M., & Wade, J. (1995). Moving on: Young people and leaving care schemes. *Social Services Review, 73*: 401–420.

Bion, W. R. (1959). Attacks on linking. In: *Second Thoughts: Selected Papers on Psychoanalysis* (pp. 93–109). London: Karnac, 1984.

Bion, W. R. (1962a). *Learning from Experience.* London: Heinemann.

Bion, W. R. (1962b). A theory of thinking. In: *Second Thoughts: Selected Papers on Psychoanalysis* (pp. 110–119). London: Karnac, 1984.

Bion, W. R. (1970). *Attention and Interpretation.* London: Tavistock.

Bor, W., Sanders, M., & Markie-Dadds, C. (2002). The effects of the Triple P-Positive Parenting Program on preschool children with co-occurring disruptive behavior and attentional/hyperactive difficulties. *Journal of Abnormal Child Psychology, 30*: 571–587.

Bowlby, J. (1988). *A Secure Base: Clinical Applications of Attachment Theory.* London: Routledge.

Breakwell, G. M., Hammond, S., & Fife-Schaw, C. (2000). *Research Methods in Psychology.* London: Sage.

Britner, P., & Phillips, D. (1995). Predictors of parent and provider satisfaction with child day care dimensions: A comparison of center-based and family child day care. *Child Welfare, 74* (6): 1135–1168.

Britton, R. (1989). The missing link: Parental sexuality in the Oedipus complex. In: R. Britton, M. Feldman, & E. O'Shaughnessy (Eds.), *The Oedipus Complex Today: Clinical Implications* (pp. 83–101). London: Karnac.

Britton, R. (1998). *Belief and Imagination: Explorations in Psychoanalysis.* London: Routledge.

Bronfenbrenner, U. (1979). *The Ecology of Human Development.* Cambridge, MA: Harvard University Press.

Browne, A. (1991). *Willy and Hugh.* London: Red Fox, 2008.

Brunning, H., Cole, C., & Huffington, C. (1997). *The Change Directory.* Richmond: Deadline Publishing.

Burck, C. (2004). Living in several languages: Implications for therapy. *Journal of Family Therapy, 26*: 314–339.

Burr, V. (1995). *An Introduction to Social Constructionism.* London: Routledge.

Byng-Hall, J. (1995). Creating a secure family base. *Family Process, 34*: 45–58.

Byng-Hall, J. (1998). Evolving ideas about narrative: Re-editing the re-editing of family mythology. *Journal of Family Therapy, 20*: 133–143.

Byng-Hall, J. (2008). Crucial roles of attachment in family therapy. *Journal of Family Therapy, 30*: 129–146.

Canham, H., & Emanuel, L. (2000). "Tied together feelings." Group psychotherapy with latency children: The process of forming a cohesive group. *Journal of Child Psychotherapy, 26* (2): 281–302.

Carter, E., & McGoldrick, M. (1989). *The Changing Family Life Cycle: Framework for Family Therapy.* New York: Allyn & Bacon.

Clough, A. H. (c. 1860). *Songs in Absence.* In: *The Poems of Arthur Hugh Clough* (2nd edition, p. 409), ed. F. L. Mulhauser. Oxford: Oxford University Press, 1974.

Cooper, P. (2001). *We Can Work It Out: What Works in Education for Pupils with Social, Emotional and Behavioural Difficulties Outside Mainstream Classrooms?* Basildon: Barnardo's.

Cousins, C. (1998). Social exclusion in Europe: Paradigms of social disadvantage in Germany, Spain, Sweden and the United Kingdom. *Politics and Policy, 26* (2): 127–146.

Cronen, V., & Pearce, W. B. (1982). The coordinated management of meaning: A theory of communication. In: F. E. Dance (Ed.), *Human Communication Theory* (pp. 60–89). New York: Harper & Row.

Dallos, R., & Draper, R. (2000). *An Introduction to Family Therapy.* Maidenhead: Open University Press.

Dartington, A. (1998). The intensity of adolescence in small families. In: R. Anderson & A. Dartington (Eds.), *Facing It Out: Clinical Perspectives on Adolescent Disturbance.* London: Duckworth.

DCSF (2008a). *Back on Track: A Strategy for Modernising Alternative Provision for Young People*. Department for Children, Schools and Families. London: HMSO.

DCSF (2008b). *Targetted Access to Mental Health Services*. Department for Children, Schools and Families. Nottingham: DCSF Publications, No. DCSF-00784-2008.

de Saint-Exupéry, A. (1943). *Le Petit Prince* [The Little Prince]. Paris: Gallimard.

DfES (1997). *When Leaving Home Is Also Leaving Care*. London: Department for Education and Skills/Social Services Inspectorate.

DfES (2003). *Every Child Matters: Change for Children* [Green Paper]. London: Department for Education and Skills.

DfES (2004). *Every Child Matters*. London: Department for Education and Skills.

DfES (2005). *Multi-Agency Working: Toolkit for Managers of Integrated Services*. Department for Education and Skills.

DfES (2006a). *Care Matters* [White Paper]. London: Department for Education and Skills.

DfES (2006b). *Developing Emotional Health and Well-Being: A Whole-School Approach to Improving Behaviour and Attendance*. London: Department for Education and Skills.

DfES (2007a). *Care Matters: Time for Change*. London: Department for Education and Skills.

DfES (2007b). *Every Parent Matters*. London: Department for Education and Skills.

Dickinson, S. (2005). *Neighbourhood Management Pathfinder Programme National Evaluation: Pathfinder Case Study*. Unpublished.

Dowling, E., & Osborne, E. (1994). *The Family and the School: A Joint Systems Approach to Problems with Children*. London: Routledge.

Erikson, E. H. (1956). The problem of ego identity. In: *Identity and the Life Cycle* (pp. 101–164). New York: International Universities Press, 1959.

Erikson, E. H. (1968). *Identity: Youth and Crisis*. New York: Norton.

Favez, N., & Métral, E. (2002). The partnership between parents and professionals in the evaluation of the development of a child with a deficiency. *Pédagogie Spécialisée*, 4: 6–11.

Favez, N., Métral, E., & Govaerts, P. (2008). Parental satisfaction with a home-based intervention for developmentally delayed children in

Switzerland: A survey over a 10-year period. *Child Care in Practice,* *14* (2): 147–163.

Fielding, M. (1999). Communities of learners—Myth: Schools are communities. In: B. O'Hagen (Ed.), *Modern Educational Myth* (pp. 64–87). London: Kogan Page.

Fivaz-Depeursinge, E., & Corboz-Warnery, A. (1999). *The Primary Triangle.* New York: Basic Books.

Foster, A., & Roberts, V. Z. (1998a). "Not in my backyard": The psychosocial reality of community care. In: A. Foster & V. Z. Roberts (Eds.), *Managing Mental Health in the Community: Chaos and Containment* (pp. 27–37). London: Routledge.

Foster, A., & Roberts, V. Z. (1998b). From understanding to action. In: A. Foster & V. Z. Roberts (Eds.), *Managing Mental Health in the Community: Chaos and Containment* (pp. 215–228). London: Routledge.

Freud, S. (1905d). *Three Essays on the Theory of Sexuality. Standard Edition, 7:* 125–245.

Fruggeri, L. (1998). *Famiglie* [Family]. Rome: Carocci Editore.

Fruggeri, L. (2002a). Genitorialità e funzione educativa in contesti triadici [Parenting and educative function in triadic contexts]. In F. Emiliani (Ed.), *I Bambini nella Vita Quotidiana. Psicologia Sociale della Prima Infanzia* [The everyday life of children: The social psychology of infants] (pp. 109–131). Rome: Carocci.

Fruggeri, L. (2002b) Different levels of analysis in the supervisory process. In: D. Campbell & B. Mason (Eds.), *Perspectives on Supervision* (pp. 3–20). London: Karnac.

Fruggeri, L. (2005a). *Families in Schools: A Network of Interdependent Agencies.* Paper presented at the first Conference on Child & Adolescent Mental Health in Educational Settings, September.

Fruggeri, L. (2005b). Sviluppo individuale e contesti familiari [Individual development and family contexts]. In: P. Bastanoni & L. Fruggeri (Eds.), *Processi di sviluppo e relazioni familiari* [Developmental process and family relations] (pp. 109–183). Milan: Unicopli.

Gergen, K. (1999). *An Invitation to Social Construction.* London: Sage.

Glaser, B., & Strauss, A. L. (1967). *The Discovery of Grounded Theory.* Chicago, IL: Aldine Publishing Company.

Glaser, D., & Prior, V. (2006). *Understanding Attachment and Attachment Disorders: Theory, Evidence and Practice.* London: Jessica Kingsley.

Glasl, F. (1994). *Konfliktmanagement. Ein Handbuch für Führungskräfte und Berater* [Conflict management: A handbook for executives and counsellors]. Stuttgart/Bern: Haupt-Verlag.

Glasl, F. (1998). *Selbsthilfe in Konflikten. Konzepte—Übungen—Praktische Methoden* [Self-help during conflicts: Concepts—training—practical methods]. Stuttgart/Bern: Haupt-Verlag.

Glisson, C., & Hemmelgarn, A. (1998). The effects of organizational climate and interorganizational coordination on the quality and outcomes of children's service systems. *Child Abuse and Neglect, 22*: 401–421.

Goleman, D. (1995). *Emotional Intelligence.* London: Bloomsbury, 1996.

Grossman, K. E., Grossman, K., & Waters, E. (Eds.) (2005). *Attachment from Infancy to Adulthood.* New York: Guilford Press.

Harré, R. (1987). *Varieties of Realism: A Rationale for the Natural Sciences.* Oxford: Blackwell.

Hartland-Rowe, L. (2005). Teaching and observing in work discussion. *International Journal of Infant Observation and Its Applications, 8* (1): 93–102.

Hinshelwood, R. D., & Skogstad, W. (2000). *Observing Organisations: Anxiety, Defence and Culture in Health Care.* London: Routledge.

Hoggett, P. (1992). *Partisans in an Uncertain World: The Psychoanalysis of Engagement.* London: Free Association Books.

Hoggett, P. (2000). *Emotional Life and the Politics of Welfare.* Basingstoke: Macmillan.

Hoxter, S. (1981). La vecchia signora che abitava in una scarpa [The old lady who lived in a shoe]. In: S. M. G. Adamo (Ed.), *Progetto Chance. Seminari scientifici* [Project Chance: Scientific seminar]. Rome: Grafica Editrice Romana.

Hudson, B. (2002). Interprofessionality in health and social care—the Achilles' heel of partnership. *Journal of Interprofessional Care, 16*: 7–17.

Huffington, C., Armstrong, D., Halton, W., Hoyle, L., & Pooley, J. (2004). *Working Below the Surface: The Emotional Life of Contemporary Organizations.* London: Karnac.

Ingrosso, M. (Ed.) (1997). *Reti di servizi e percorsi degli utenti in due sistemi socio-educativi* [Network of services and consumers' pathways in two socio-educative systems]. Bologne: Regione Emilia-Romagna, Assessorato ai Servizi Sociali.

Jackson, E. (2002). Mental health in schools: What about the staff? *Journal of Child Psychotherapy, 28* (2): 129–146.

Joseph Rowntree Foundation (1997). Black families' survival strategies: Ways of coping in UK society. *Findings. Social Policy Research, 135*. [York: Joseph Rowntree Foundation.]

Kegerreis, S. (1995). Getting better makes it worse. In: J. Trowell & M. Bower (Eds.), *The Emotional Needs of Young Children and Their Families: Using Psychoanalytical Ideas in the Community* (pp. 101–108). London: Routledge.

Kenrick, J., Lindsey, C., & Tollemache, L. (2006). *Creating New Families.* London: Karnac.

Klein, M. (1924). The role of the school in the libidinal development of the child. *International Journal of Psychoanalysis, 5*: 312–331.

Klein, M. (1946). Notes on some schizoid mechanisms. *International Journal of Psychoanalysis, 27*: 99–110.

Klein, M. (1959). Our adult world and its roots in infancy. *Human Relations, 12*: 291–303.

Kuhlmann, B., & Rieforth, J. (2004). Das Neun-Felder-Modell. Strategisch-lösungsorientiertes Vorgehen im Meditationsprozess [The Nine-Field Model: A strategic-orientated approach to the meditation process]. *Zeitschrift für Konfliktmanagement, 2.*

Kuhlmann, B., & Rieforth, J. (2006). Pathogenese, Salutogenese und Triadisches Verstehen—Das Neun-Felder-Modell. Ein lösungsorientiertes Verfahren in Therapie und Beratung [Pathogenesis, salutogenesis, and triadic understanding—The Nine-Field Model: A solution-oriented technique for therapy and counselling]. In: J. Rieforth (Ed.), *Triadisches Verstehen in sozialen Systemen* [Triadic understanding in social systems]. Heidelberg: Carl-Auer-Verlag.

Laming, Lord H. (2003). *The Victoria Climbié Inquiry—Report of an Inquiry.* London: TSO.

Lanners, R., & Mombaerts, D. (2000). Evaluation of parents' satisfaction with early intervention services within and among European countries: Construction and application of a new parent satisfaction scale. *Infants and Young Children, 12* (3): 61–70.

Lawrence, D. H. (1928). *Lady Chatterley's Lover.* Florence: Orioli. Signet Classic edition.

Leigh, M. (Dir.) (2004). *Vera Drake.* A Thin Man Films/Les Films Alain Sade Production. London: Thin Man Films.

Lindsey, C. (1993). Family systems reconstructed in the mind of the systemic therapist. *Human Systems, 4*: 299–310.

Lloyd, G., Stead, J., & Kendrick, A. (2001). *Hanging On in There: A*

Study of Inter-Agency Work to Prevent School Exclusion in Three Local Authorities. London: National Children's Bureau.

Maitra, B. (2006). Culture and the mental health of children: The "cutting edge" of expertise. In: S. Timimi & B. Maitra (Eds.), *Critical Voices in Child and Adolescent Mental Health*. London: Free Association Books.

McQuail, S., & Pugh, G. (1995). *Effective Organisation of Early Childhood Services*. London: National Children's Bureau.

Mehta, P. (1997). The import and export of psychoanalysis: India. *Journal of the American Academy of Psychoanalysis, 25*: 455–472.

Meltzel, H., Gatward, R., Curbin, T., Goodman, R., & Ford, T. (2003). *The Mental Health of Young People Looked After by Local Authorities in England*. London: TSO.

Menzies Lyth, I. (1959). The functioning of social systems as a defence against anxiety: A report on a study of the nursing service of a general hospital. In: *Containing Anxiety in Institutions: Selected Essays* (pp. 43–85). London: Free Association Books, 1988.

Mikardo, J. (1996). Hate in the countertransference. *Journal of Child Psychotherapy, 22* (3): 398–401.

Miller, E. J., & Rice, A. K. (1967). Task and sentient systems and their boundary controls. In: *Systems of Organization* (pp. 251–270). London: Tavistock Publications. Reprinted in: E. Trist & H. Murray (Eds.), *The Social Engagement of Social Science, Vol. 1: The Socio-Psychological Perspective* (pp. 259–271). London: Free Association Books, 1990.

Minuchin, S. (1974). *Families and Family Therapy*. Cambridge, MA: Harvard University Press.

Montada, L., & Kals, E. (2007). *Mediation. Lehrbuch für Psychologen und Juristen* [Mediation: A textbook for psychologists and lawyers]. Weinheim: Beltz Psychologie Verlags Union (PVU).

Mosse, J., & Roberts, V. Z. (1994). Finding a voice: Differentiation, representation and empowerment in organisations under threat. In: A. Obholzer & V. Z. Roberts (Eds.), *The Unconscious at Work: Individual and Organisational Stress in the Human Services* (pp. 147–155). London: Routledge.

Nandy, A. (1983). *The Intimate Enemy: Loss and Recovery of Self under Colonialism*. Oxford: Oxford University Press.

Nashat, S. (2008). *Exploring Professional Responses to Children with Emotional and Behavioural Difficulties: A Comparative Study of Mental*

Health and Education Professionals. Unpublished manuscript, Tavistock Clinic.

Neuberger, R. (2005). *Le mythe familial* [The family myth]. Paris: ESF Editeurs.

OFSTED (2003). Education in special schools and pupil referral units. In: *Annual Report of Her Majesty's Chief Inspector of Schools: Standards and Quality in Education 2002/03.* Office for Standards in Education, Children's Services and Skills. London: HMSO.

OFSTED (2007). *Pupil Referral Units: Establishing Successful Practice in Pupil Referral Units and Local Authorities.* Office for Standards in Education, Children's Services and Skills. London: HMSO.

Osgood, J., & Sharp, C. (2000). Developing early education and childcare services for the 21st century. In: *LGA Research Report, 12.* Slough: National Foundation for Educational Research.

Paiva, N. D. (2005). *I Am from Here: The Unclear Boundaries for Young Bangladeshis Growing Up in London.* Paper presented at the First European Conference on Child & Adolescent Mental Health in Educational Settings, Paris, 22–23 September.

Papadopoulos, R. (1998). Storied community as a secure base. *British Journal of Psychotherapy*, 15: 322–332

Parsons, C. (1999). *Education, Exclusion and Citizenship.* London: Routledge.

Payne, M. (2000). *Narrative Therapy: An Introduction for Counsellors.* London: Sage.

Pearce, W. B. (2007). *Making Social Worlds: A Communication Perspective.* Oxford: Blackwell Publishing.

Pearce, W. B., & Cronen, V. E. (1980). *Communication, Action, and Meaning.* New York: Praeger.

Philipp, E., & Rademacher, H. (2002). *Konfliktmanagement im Kollegium. Arbeitsbuch mit Modellen und Methoden.* [Conflict management between members of staff: An exercise book with models and methods]. Weinheim: Beltz.

Potter, J., & Wetherell, M. (2007). *Discourse and Social Psychology* (7th edition). London: Sage.

Reed, B. D., & Palmer, B. W. M. (1972). *An Introduction to Organisational Behaviour.* London: Grubb Institute.

Rendall, S., & Stuart, M. (2005). *Excluded from School: Systemic Practice for Mental Health and Education Professionals.* London: Routledge.

Roberts, V. Z. (1994). The organisation of work: Contributions from open systems theory. In: A. Obholzer & V. Z. Roberts (Eds.), *The Unconscious at Work: Individual and Organisational Stress in the Human Services* (pp. 28–38). London: Routledge.

Rustin, M. (2005). *Discussion of S. M. G. Adamo's Paper: "Fox's Earth: the Potential of a Project"*. Paper presented at Conference on New Educational Services for Early Childhood from Present to Future, Castel dell'Ovo, Naples.

Rustin, M. (2008). Introduction. In: M. Rustin & J. Bradley (Eds.), *Work Discussion: Learning from Reflective Practice in Work with Children and Families* (pp. xxiii–xxvi). London: Karnac.

Rustin, M., & Bradley, J. (Eds.) (2008). *Work Discussion: Learning from Reflective Practice in Work with Children and Families*. London: Karnac.

Rutter, M. (1999). Resilience concepts and findings: Implications for family therapy. *Journal of Family Therapy, 21*: 119–144.

Salmon, G. (2004). Multi-agency collaboration: The challenges for CAMHS. *Child and Adolescent Mental Health, 9* (4): 156–161.

Salmon, G., & Faris, J. (2006). Multi-agency collaboration, multiple levels of meanings: Social construction and the CMM model as tools to further our understanding. *Journal of Family Therapy, 28* (3): 272–292.

Salzberger-Wittenberg, I. (1970). *Psychoanalytic Insights and Relationships: A Kleinian Approach*. London: Routledge & Kegan Paul.

Salzberger-Wittenberg, I., Henry, G., & Osborne, E. (1983). *The Emotional Experience of Learning and Teaching*. London: Routledge & Kegan Paul.

Settlage, C. F. (1991). On the treatment of preoedipal pathology. In: S. Akhtar & H. Parens (Eds.), *Beyond the Symbiotic Orbit: Advances in Separation–Individuation Theory: Essays in Honor of Selma Kramer MD* (pp. 350–357). Hillsdale, NJ: Analytic Press.

Sharp, P. (2001). *Nurturing Emotional Literacy*. London: David Fulton.

Shengold, L. (1989). *The Effects of Childhood Abuse and Deprivation*. New Haven, CT: Yale University Press.

Shotter, J. (2000). *Conversational Realities: Constructing Life through Language*. London: Sage.

Simpson, P., & French, R. (2005). Thoughtful leadership. *Organisational and Social Dynamics, 5* (2): 280–297.

Sinason, V. (1992). *Mental Handicap and the Human Condition: New Approaches from the Tavistock*. London: Free Association.

Slee, R. (1998). Inclusive education? This must signify "new times" in educational research. *British Journal of Educational Studies, 46* (4): 440–454.

Spratley, J., & Pietroni, M. (1994). *Creative Collaboration: Interprofessional Learning Priorities in Primary Health and Community Care.* Report of a project undertaken by Marylebone Centre Trust on behalf of CCETSW. London: Marylebone Centre Trust.

Steiner, J. (1985). Turning a blind eye: The cover up for Oedipus. *International Review of Psychoanalysis, 12*: 161–172.

Stern, D. (1985). *The Interpersonal World of the Infant.* New York: Basic Books.

Stierlin, H. (2001). *Psychoanalyse—Familientherapie—Systemische Therapie.* [Psychoanalysis—Family therapy—Systemic therapy]. Stuttgart: Klett-Cotta.

Sweet, M., & Appelbaum, M. (2004). Is home visiting an effective strategy? A meta-analytic review of home visiting programs for families with young children. *Child Development, 75* (5): 1435–1456.

Thomas, A., & Chess, S. (1977). *Temperament and Development.* New York: Brunner/Mazel

Townsley, R., Abbott, D., & Watson, D. (2004). *Making a Difference? Exploring the Impact of Multi-Agency Working on Disabled Children with Complex Health Care Needs, Their Families and the Professionals Who Support Them.* Bristol: Policy Press.

Urwin, C. (2003). Breaking ground, hitting ground: A Sure Start rapid response service for parents and their under fours. *Journal of Child Psychotherapy, 29* (3): 375–392.

Urwin, C. (2007). Doing infant observation differently? Researching the formation of mothering identities in an Inner London borough. *International Journal of Infant Observation, 10* (3): 239–252.

Von Schlippe, A., & Schweitzer, J. (1996). *Lehrbuch der systemischen Therapie und Beratung* [Textbook of systemic therapy and counselling]. Göttingen: Vandenhoeck & Ruprecht.

Waddell, M. (2002). *Inside Lives.* London: Karnac.

Waddell, M. (2005). *Understanding 12–14 Year Olds.* London: Jessica Kingsley.

Warmington, P., Daniels, H., Edwards, A., Brown, S., Leadbetter, J., Martin, D., et al. (2004). *Interagency Collaboration: A Review of the Literature.* Birmingham: University of Birmingham/Economic Social Research Council.

Weare, K. (2000). *Promoting Mental, Emotional and Social Health: A Whole School Approach*. London: Routledge.

Webster-Stratton, C., & Mostyn, D. (1992). *The Incredible Years: A Troubles-Shooting Guide for Parents of Children Aged 3–8*. Toronto: Umbrella Press.

Webster-Stratton, C., & Reid, M. J. (2003). The Incredible Years parents, teachers and children training series: A multifaceted treatment approach for young children with conduct problems. In: A. E. Kazdin & J. R. Weisz (Eds.), *Evidence-Based Psychotherapies for Children and Adolescents* (pp. 224–240). London: Guilford Press.

White, M. (2007). *Maps of Narrative Practice*. New York: Norton.

White, M., & Epston, D. (1990). *Narrative Means to Therapeutic Ends*. New York: Norton.

Williams, G. (1997). *Internal Landscapes and Foreign Bodies*. London: Duckworth.

Winnicott, D. W. (1958). The capacity to be alone. *International Journal of Psychoanalysis, 39*: 416–420.

Winnicott, D. W. (1965). *The Maturational Processes and the Facilitating Environment*. London: Hogarth Press.

Winnicott, D. W. (1971). *Playing and Reality*. London: Routledge.

Wittgenstein, L. (1922). *Tractatus Logico-Philosophicus* (2nd edition). London: Routledge, 2001.

Youell, B. (2006). *The Learning Relationship*. London: Karnac.

Zay, D. (2005). *Prévenir l'exclusion scolaire et sociale des jeunes. Une approche Franco-Britannique* [Preventing school and social exclusion of young people: A Franco–British approach]. Paris: Presses Universitaires de France.

INDEX